The Mood of Christmas

The
Mood of Christmas

HOWARD THURMAN

HARPER & ROW, PUBLISHERS
New York, Evanston, San Francisco, London

The selections listed below originally appeared in the following books by Howard Thurman:

The Centering Moment. Copyright © 1969 by Howard Thurman.
Christmas; The Common Mood; We Are Visited; We want to Be Understood

Deep Is the Hunger. Copyright 1951 by Harper & Row.
The Art of Grace; Gift of Imagination; The Gift of Memory; Grace at Meat; The Idiom of Brotherhood; Life's Working Paper; Magic All Around Us; "Make Me Big"; Moments of Complete Joy; The New Year; The Place Where You Live; The Point of Greatest Need; A Prayer of Old Age; The Self-giving Impulse; A Sense of Fancy; The Will to Understand; Your Joy

Disciplines of the Spirit. Copyright © 1963 by Howard Thurman.
Life Becomes Personal

Footprints of a Dream. Copyright © 1959 by Howard Thurman.
Madonna and Child

The Greatest of These. Copyright 1944 by Howard Thurman.
The Great Incarnate Word

The Inward Journey. Copyright © 1961 by Howard Thurman.
The Binding Unity; But Then Face to Face; The Experience of Love; For We Know in Part; Friends Whom I Knew Not; Given Element in Life; The Good Deed; In His Image; The Integrity of the Person; Joy Is of Many Kinds; Knowledge . . . Shall Vanish Away; Let Us Remember the Children; Making a Good Life; The Miracle of Living; A Moment Becomes *the* Moment; The Night View of the World; A Prayer for Peace; The Sacrament of Remembrance; To Him That Waits; To Rise to the Great Occasion; Twilights and Endless Landscapes; Your Loneliness

Meditations of the Heart. Copyright 1953 by Harper & Row.
Against the Background of the Year; Blessings at Year's End; The Desert Dweller; The Experience of Growing Up; The Glad Surprise; A Gracious Spirit; A New Melody; Keep Alive the Dream in the Heart; Life, an Offering to God; Life Seems Unaware; Lord Open Unto Me; Men Cannot be Indifferent to Men; No Man Is an Island; Our Children Are Not *Things*; Our Little Lives; The Sacrament of Christmas; The Season of Remembrance; The Strange Irony; She Practices Brotherhood; Teach Me Thy Grace; This Is a New Year; To What Loyalty Are You True?; We Are All One

Designed by C. Linda Dingler

Library of Congress Cataloging in Publication Data

Thurman, Howard, 1899-
The mood of Christmas.
Includes selections from the author's previous works.
1. Christmas—Meditations. I. Title.
BV45.T46   242'.33   73-6332
ISBN 0-06-068051-2

Acknowledgments

To Alice Ratner, my secretary, without whose careful work, far beyond the ordinary demand, this manuscript could not have been prepared

To Elizabeth Ballard, Marsh Chapel, Boston University, for making available material from previous Chapel Bulletins

To various friends who provided materials written at other times and other places

Contents

The Preface   xi

The Prologue   1

The Reaches of the Past   5
The Historic Root 5—The Hope of the Disinherited 9—The Singing of Angels 10—The Graces of Christmas 11—

The Madonna and Child   13

The Christmas Greeting   17
I Will Light Candles This Christmas 19—The Christmas Candles 19—This Is Christmas 20—Christmas Is Yesterday 20—Christmas Is Waiting to Be Born 21—Christmas Is the Season of the Heart 21—Christmas Returns 22—Gifts on My Altar 22—The Growing Edge 23—The Work of Christmas 23—I Will Sing a New Song 24—Christmas Is the Season of Affirmation 24—At Christmastime 25—This Is the Season of Promise 25—The Sacrament of Christmas 26—The Season of Remembrance 26—Against the Background of the Year 27—Life Seems Unaware 28—

Christmas Meditations   29
A Moment Is *the* Moment: Part I 31—A Moment Is *the* Moment: Part II 32—"But Then Face to

Face" 33—The Gift of Grace 35—The Seasons of God 36—The Good Deed 38—To Share the Best 39—Awareness of Another's Need 40—The Point of Greatest Need 41—A Unique Christmas Story 42—In His Image 44—Grace at Meat 45 —The Self-giving Impulse 47—The Art of Grace 47—The Gift of Memory 48—The Gift of Imagination 49—Life, an Offering to God 50—The Desert Dweller 51—Given Element in Life 52—The Binding Unity 53—The Strange Irony 54—The Idiom of Brotherhood 54—The Will to Understand 55—"Friends Whom I Knew Not" 56— "We Are All One" 57—She Practices Brotherhood 58—"No Man Is an Island" 59—"For We Know in Part" 61—The Strange Glory 62—Life Becomes Personal 63—Our Little Lives 64—When the Strain Is Heaviest 65—Lord, Lord, Open Unto Me 65—Making a Good Life 66—New Wood 67— "Knowledge . . . Shall Vanish Away" 68—The Integrity of the Person 70—Life's Working Paper 71 —"Make Me Big" 72—A Sense of Fancy 73—The Place Where You Live 74—Keep Alive the Dream in the Heart 75—To Which Loyalty Are You True? 76—The Experience of Growing Up 77—The Glad Surprise 78—Man Cannot Be Indifferent to Men 79—The Quickening Possibility 80—The Climate of Acceptance 81—We Want to Be Understood 82—We Are Visited 83—"Magic All Around Us" 84—The Experience of Love 85—Let Us Remember the Children 86—The Sacrament of Remembrance 87—Our Children Are Not *Things* 88—Twilights and Endless Landscapes 89—To Be Secure 91— Joy Is of Many Kinds 92—Moments of Complete Joy 93—Your Joy 94—"To Him That Waits" 95 —Your Loneliness 96—"The Night View of the World" 97—The Miracle of Living 98—"A Gracious Spirit" 99—Teach Me Thy Grace 100—A Prayer for Peace 100—We Behold Our Lives 101— The Ceiling of Thy Hopes I Will Lift on High 103 —A Prayer of Old Age 104—A New Melody 105— The Common Mood 106—Christmas 107—To Rise to the Great Occasion 108—

The Great Incarnate Words   109

    The Great Incarnate Words   111—

The End of the Year   119

    End of the Year   121—Blessings at Year's End   123
    —This Is a New Year   124—The New Year   125—

The Epilogue   129

The Preface

There is a need in the human spirit for the salutation of life. It is the act of celebration that provides a personal and collective awareness of the place and significance of the individual in the continuity, in the flow of life itself. This sense of continuity is the ultimate windbreak against the ever-present threat of isolation and separation from the surrounding environ. The most natural thing is that the individual life would seem to be a part of the drama of events taking place in nature. Hardly can we imagine the impact in the life of the man who first responded to the coming of the dawn by saying "Day breaks."

The celebration of Christmas belongs in such a sequence. It is a matter of record that the birth of Jesus cannot be established as to the exact date. There is general agreement that the spirit of Christmas is associated with symbols long identified with the winter solstice. But such considerations are beside the point because the season itself is a part of the rhythm of nature of which mankind is a part. They highlight the fact that there is a mood of remembrance and sheer rejoicing that is memorialized in the flow of the season itself.

In the pages that follow there are many gentle sharings of the religious spirit apotheosized in the Christian interpretation of the Christmas season. For this we affirm our solidarity with the whole human race in its long struggle to become humane and to reveal the divinity in which all mankind shares. Therefore, when we build our crèche, light our special candles, decorate the evergreen with tinsel and color, hold our romantic tryst under the mistletoe, prepare the festive meal, share our gifts as a celebration of the privacy and universality of love, take the time to remember in many ways those who touched us in the midst of the traffic of the commonplace and sing the ancient carols in honor of the birth of Him who was "the sign of man's attack"—when we do these things we show that God has not left Himself without specific witness to His love and care of us as His children. To the strong and the weak, to the happy and the sorrowful, to the barren and the fruitful womb, to the devout believer and the arrogant unbeliever, to the Christian and the non-Christian, there is the ever-present hope that tidings of great joy will find their way into the heart and life.

These pages follow a simple outline: A Prologue, which has to do with the Mood of Christmas. This is followed by the perspective of history in which Jesus released a precious ingredient into the psychic stream of the human race. There is a tribute to the Madonna and Child, then a rendering of a series of Christmas greetings, many of which have had a very wide, intensive circulation. The longest section deals with meditative writings depicting the range of moods incident to the human condition but expressive of direct and indirect overtones of healing words appropriate to the season. There is a rather extensive prose-poem which gathers into its focus a statement of the gift which the Master's life shares with all who wrestle with Fear, Deception, and Hate in their effort to live lives worthy of children of men and children of God. Since the Christmas season also marks the end of the year, recognition of this fact seems most appropriate. Finally, there is a short Epilogue which brings into a single creative synthesis the impact of the life of Jesus whose birth is celebrated by the Christmas season.

The Prologue

*C*hristmas is a mood, a quality, a symbol. It is never merely a fact. As a fact it is a date on the calendar—to the believer it is the anniversary of an event in human history. An individual may relate himself meaningfully to the fact or the event, but that would not be Christmas.

The mood of Christmas—what is it? It is a quickening of the presence of other human beings into whose lives a precious part of one's own has been released. It is a memory of other days when into one's path an angel appeared spreading a halo over an ordinary moment or a commonplace event. It is an iridescence of sheer delight that bathes one's whole being with something more wonderful than words can ever tell. Of such is the mood of Christmas.

The quality of Christmas—what is it? It is the fullness with which fruit ripens, blossoms unfold into flowers, and live coals glow in the darkness. It is the richness of vibrant colors—the calm purple of grapes, the exciting redness of tomatoes, the shimmering light on the noiseless stirring of a lake or sunset. It is the sense of plateau with a large rock behind which one may take temporary respite from winds that chill. Of such is the quality of Christmas.

The symbol of Christmas—what is it? It is the rainbow arched over the roof of the sky when the clouds are heavy with foreboding. It is the cry of life in the newborn babe when, forced from its mother's nest, it claims its right to live. It is the brooding Presence of the Eternal Spirit making crooked paths straight, rough places smooth, tired hearts refreshed, dead hopes stir with newness of life. It is the promise of tomorrow at the close of every day, the movement of life in defiance of death, and the assurance that love is sturdier than hate, that right is more confident than wrong, that good is more permanent than evil.

The
Reaches of the Past

The Historic Root

The trained mind when brought face to face with the mystery of Jesus has no choice but to seek to reduce it to a manageable unit of comprehension in order to understand it. In other words, it has to make sense. This is a legitimate and inescapable demand. One profoundly significant and primary consideration must be held steadily in mind as the historical quest is pursued.

Despite all the merit that there is in the scholarly and reverential researches into the facts concerning the historical Jesus, they do not, nor can they, explain him adequately. A spiritual genius, or any kind of genius for that matter, cannot ever be explained in any complete sense. This is true whether the exploration is in terms of his historical setting, his psychological pattern, or his social, biological, and religious heritage. Uniqueness is continually elusive; no explanation can compass why Jesus differs from those others whom the same explanation would fit.

Any explanation of Jesus in terms of the social or economic forces of his time must inevitably explain his contemporaries as well. Such analysis may explain why he was a particular kind of Jew, for instance, but it does not explain why the other Jews were not Jesus. What is most compelling about him is not so much the way in which he resembled his fellows, but the way in which he differed from all the rest of them.

It is reasonable to suppose that Jesus inherited the same traits as countless other Jews of his time. He grew up in the same society, the same traditions, pinnacled on the same funded prophetic insight, yet he was Jesus and the others were not. Often we seek refuge in history or psychology or economics and we are reluctant to face the problem remaining when history or psychology or economics has done its uttermost. All three disciplines, and others, are useful in their way; the tragedy is in forgetting what that way is. To quote a young sociologist* who died long before high noon: "The scientific mood does not imply that other moods are fatuous or futile; it does not hold that the truths it enables men to discover are the only truths. . . . he [the scientist] knows too well that behind the symbols of mathematics and the formulae of chemistry and physics and the rigid generalizations of psychology and social sciences lie the unexplained mysteries of twilight and music, of autumn nights fringed with silver, of human fortitude and idealism."

How may a critical mind adjust itself to what remains as an irreducible, inescapable residuum about Jesus Christ? One contemporary New Testament scholar says, "Some may come to faith in God and to love, without a conscious attachment to Jesus. Both nature and good men besides Jesus may lead us to God. They who seek God with all their hearts must, however, some day on their way meet Jesus."**

At long last there is no successful argument against a life. The word "myth" has been used to cover the inexplicable aspects of Jesus and the ground of his amazing revelation of the life of God. But the word "myth" is used most profoundly in "its older meaning, representing something that is not strictly science, history or philosophy, but is the attempt to set forth in practical form what is felt to be above and beyond expression in the categories of formal thought."

Jesus did create in men a faith in himself as one who had a primary experience of the heart of God. Perhaps he did not walk on the water, perhaps he did not turn water to wine, perhaps he did none of the miraculous things ascribed to him, but his contemporaries said he did these things. That fact is a tremendous revelation of the astounding proportions of his stature.

If God is and if He is love, as I believe most profoundly, and if in Jesus there is the projection of this central affirmation in concrete flesh and blood, then in such a person there are inevitably precious clues as to the meaning of God and the meaning of life. His way of life, then, becomes *the* way of life at its highest and best.

Thus the historical quest throws important light upon the central figure of the Christmas story.

* Russell Gordon Smith.

** Heinrich Weinel and Alban Widgery, *Jesus in the Nineteenth Century and After*, p. 405.

The Hope of the Disinherited

In the Book it is written that Simeon was a Jew full of years, who had hoped so long for Israel that his hope created the thing upon which it had fed. He said, "This child is destined for the downfall as well as for the rise of many a one in Israel; destined to be a Sign for man's attack—to bring out the secret aims of many a heart" (Moffatt). Simeon in a sense is the symbol of the disinherited looking for the consolation of Israel. He felt that the Christ child was the answer. Was he right?

In seeking to answer that question, certain facts are of profound significance. Jesus was poor. He was not a Roman citizen like Paul and was therefore outside the circle of real privilege. He was a carpenter. He did not write a book. He did not travel very far from his home. He was tender without being soft. He was kind without being sentimental. He was gracious without being officious. He refused to be made into a political leader and resisted the pressure to become merely a popular hero.

He came preaching a message of hope. Its predominant note was not eschatological. But he understood its meaning. He knew that the otherworldly hope is the cry of pain of the human spirit as it writhes in the toils of an overmastering frustration. He knew also that it gave relief to the human spirit—temporary but mighty. It is temporary because it affirms a complete and thoroughgoing dualism and affirms the ultimate defeat of God in the world of men. His faith in God could not let that pass unchallenged. He knew further that at the heart of such a hope there is not only despair but also deep revenge and the completest invalidation of the unity of life. Eschatology deals in antitheses but scarcely in syntheses. The failure to see this is one of the profoundest illusions of the dispossessed. Over against that, Jesus insists that God is the God of the just and the unjust. Ultimately, this is God's world and He can never be God in this world if He bowed finally before the swirling, seething cauldron of oppression and injustice in the world.

His message was one of love as against hate and bitterness. He was never more of a realist than at this point. Hate is powerful; often his followers have been very sentimental in their shallow and unthoughtout repudiations. Hate is apt to be for the oppressed a sure but temporary form of validation. When the disinherited cannot fight, cannot even struggle, caught and trapped by the iron hands of unconscious or reflective injustice, hate crystallizes the personality and makes it possible for a vast defiance to be flung into the teeth of the destroyer. But Jesus said that this finally burned out all the spiritual bearings in the life of the hater and left him a charred corpse, stranded on the shores of his desolate experience. He knew that love was the most completely persistent quality of which the human spirit is capable, because for its sake and under its aegis men will do gladly what no power in heaven or hell could make them do without love.

Fundamental to all was his deep confidence in God. This is the heart of what he gives to the disinherited. Here is no superficial optimism, but a vast faith that reaches through all the dimensions of human life, giving dignity, worth, and purpose even to the least significant. In Jesus, all men may see the illumined finger of God guiding them in the way that they should go, so that high above the clash of arms in the conflict for status, for place, for privilege, for rights, he can hear speaking distinctly and clearly to his own spirit the still small voice of God, without which nothing has real meaning, with which all the rest of the journey, however difficult, however painful, however devastating, will be filled with a music all its own and even the stars in their appointed rounds and all the wooded world of nature participate in the triumphant music of his heart.

Such is the faith he communicates, and in its presence even Death becomes a little thing.

The Singing of Angels

There must be always remaining in every man's life some place for the singing of angels—some place for that which in itself is breathlessly beautiful and by an inherent prerogative throwing all the rest of life into a new and created relatedness. Something that gathers up in itself all the freshets of experience from drab and commonplace areas of living and glows in one bright white light of penetrating beauty and meaning—then passes. The commonplace is shot through now with new glory—old burdens become lighter, deep and ancient wounds lose much of their old, old hurting. A crown is placed over our heads that for the rest of our lives we are trying to grow tall enough to wear. Despite all of the crassness of life, despite all of the hardness of life, despite all of the harsh discords of life, life is saved by the singing of angels.

* * *

Oscar Wilde says in his *De Profundis*, There is always room in an ignorant man's mind for a great idea. It is of profoundest significance to me that the Gospel story, particularly in the Book of Luke, reveals that the announcement of the birth of Jesus comes first to simple shepherds who were about their appointed tasks. After theology has done its work, after the reflective judgments of men from the heights and lonely retreats of privilege and security have wrought their perfect patterns, the birth of Jesus remains the symbol of the dignity and the inherent worthfulness of the common man.

Stripped bare of art forms and liturgy, the literal substance of the story remains, Jesus Christ was born in a stable, he was born of humble parentage in surroundings that are the common lot of those who earn their living by the sweat of their brows. Nothing can rob the common man of this heritage—when he beholds Jesus, he sees in him the possibilities of life even for the humblest and a dramatic resolution of the meaning of God.

If the theme of the angels' song is to find fulfillment in the world, it will be through the common man's becoming aware of his true worthfulness and asserting his generic prerogatives as a child of God. The diplomats, the politicians, the statesmen, the lords of business and religion will never bring peace in the world. Violence is the behavior pattern of Power in the modern world, and violence has its own etiquette and ritual, and its own morality.

The Graces of Christmas

For many devout Christians all over the world, December 25 marks a dramatic moment in the series of dramatic moments by which the will of God has manifest itself within the time-space involvements of human life. They regard the birth of Jesus as a moment when God was introduced into time in the form of this incarnation. Many other

Christians are sure that this day marks the birth of a baby who grew up to be a good man, one of the best men who ever lived—a man who in tenderness, in graciousness, and in sensitivity set a new record for the meaning and the worth of the individual. Many others regard him as one who came into the world as anyone else comes into the world, and as the result of the way he lived and the intensity of his experience of God, he became more and more available to the mind and the spirit and to the will of God, and he achieved a sonship which was not his at birth.

It doesn't matter from one point of view which one of these orientations is yours, or it matters a great deal. But the important thing is that to the mother of Jesus he was a baby boy who grew hungry, who had to be fed, bathed, nurtured, who had to be given tender loving care, one who pulled at her heartstrings and who became so much a part of her sense of worth and meaning that she was sure, in a sense, that this was the first baby in the world. And perhaps every mother feels, particularly about her first baby, that this is the first—this is the original baby—and this can be understood.

The story of Christmas has certain very simple human things in it which appeal to my kind of mind and spirit. A family—a man, a woman, a child—animals, simple surroundings, the primary family unit. There is always the possibility that the first steps in love, in trust, in confidence, can be measured, developed, expanded. So that when we think of Christmas, let us think of it as a time when we remember the graces of life. It is important to seize upon the atmosphere created during this period, to let it tutor our own spirits in kindness and in imaginative sympathy. Thus we may be able to give ourselves freely to the babies in our midst, to sustain them in their growth into youth and maturity. We must do our part to guarantee that all children may have the chance to be children, to experience their own childhood. If this does not happen to them, they will be forced to deal with their environment as if they were adults. There can be no good future for mankind if this sensitivity to the birth and meaning of the child that we see in Christmas is ignored.

The
Madonna and Child

Madonna and Child

During the season of Christmas in many art galleries, in countless homes and churches, and on myriad Christmas cards, there will be scenes picturing the Madonna and Child. There is a sense in which the Madonna and Child experience is not the exclusive possession of any faith or any race. This is not to gainsay, to underestimate, or to speak irreverently of the far-reaching significance of the Madonna in Christianity, particularly in Roman Catholicism. But it is to point out the fact that the Madonna and Child both in art and religion is a recognition of the universality of the experience of motherhood as an expression of the creative and redemptive principle of life. It affirms the constancy of the idea that life is dynamic and alive—that death as the final consummation of life is an illusion.

The limitless resources of life are at the disposal of the creative impulse that fulfills itself most intimately and profoundly in the experience of the birth of a child. Here the mother becomes one with the moving energy of existence—in the experience of birth there is neither time, nor space, nor individuality, nor private personal existence—she is absorbed in a vast creative moment upon which the continuity of the race is dependent. The experience itself knows no race, no culture, no language—it is the trysting place of woman and the Eternal.

The Madonna and Child in Christianity is profoundly rooted in this background of universality. Specifically, it dramatizes the birth of a Jewish baby, under unique circumstances, calling attention to a destiny in which the whole human race is involved. For many to whom he is the Savior of mankind, no claim as to his origin is too great or too lofty. Here is the culmination of a vast expectancy and the fulfillment of a desperate need. Through the ages the message of him whose coming is celebrated at Christmastime says again and again through artists, through liturgy, through music, through the written and spoken word, through great devotion and heroic sacrifice, that the destiny of man on the earth is a good and common destiny —that however dark the moment or the days may be, the redemptive impulse of God is ever present in human life.

But there is something more. The Madonna and Child conception suggests that the growing edge of human life, the hope of every generation, is in the birth of the child. The stirring of the child in the womb is the perennial sign of man's attack on bigotry, blindness, prejudice, greed, hate, and all the host of diseases that make of man's life a nightmare and a holocaust.

The Birth of the Child in China, Japan, the Philippines, Russia, India, America, and all over the world, is the breathless moment like the stillness of absolute motion, when something new, fresh, whole, may be ushered into the nations that will be the rallying point for the whole human race to move in solid phalanx into the city of God, into the Kingdom of Heaven on the earth . . .

The
Christmas Greeting

T he true meaning of Christmas is expressed in the sharing of one's graces in a world in which it is so easy to become callous, insensitive, and hard. Once this spirit becomes part of a man's life, every day is Christmas, and every night is freighted with anticipation of the dawning of fresh, and perhaps holy, adventure.

I Will Light Candles This Christmas

Candles of joy, despite all sadness,
Candles of hope where despair keeps watch.
Candles of courage for fears ever present,
Candles of peace for tempest-tossed days,
Candles of grace to ease heavy burdens,
Candles of love to inspire all my living,
Candles that will burn all the year long.

The Christmas Candles

I will light the candle of fellowship this Christmas. I know that the experiences of unity in human relations are more compelling than the concepts, the fears, the prejudices, which divide. Despite the tendency to feel my race superior, my nation the greatest nation, my faith the true faith, I must beat down the boundaries of my exclusiveness until my sense of separateness is completely enveloped in a sense of fellowship. There must be free and easy access by all, to all the rich resources accumulated by groups and individuals in years of living and experiencing. I will light the candle of fellowship this Christmas, a candle that must burn all the year long.

I will light the candle of hope this Christmas. There is strange irony in the fact that there seems to exist a more secure basis for hope in the world during the grimmest days of war than in the vast uncertainties of peace. The miracle of fulfillment dreamed of by the uprooted and persecuted masses of men, women, and children takes now the form of a hideous nightmare, as peace is so long deferred. But hope is the mood of Christmas: the raw materials are a newborn babe, a family, and work. Life keeps coming on, keeps seeking to fulfill itself, keeps affirming the possibility of hope.

This Is Christmas

The evergreen singing aloud its poem of constant renewal,
The festive mood spreading lilting magic everywhere,
The gifts of recollection calling to heart the graces of life,
The star in the sky calling to mind the wisdom of hope,
The warmth of candlelight glowing against the darkness,
The birth of a child linking past to future,
The symbol of love absorbing all violence.
                    THIS IS CHRISTMAS

Christmas Is Yesterday:

The memories of childhood,
The miracle of Santa Claus,
The singing of carols—
The glow of being remembered.

Christmas Is Today:

The presence of absent ones,
The reminder of the generous act,
The need to love—
The need to be loved.

Christmas Is Tomorrow:

The miracle of faith,
The fulfillment of ancient hopes,
The reign of God—
The dying of Death in the land.
Christmas is yesterday, today, and tomorrow.

Christmas Is Waiting to Be Born:

Where refugees seek deliverance that never comes,
And the heart consumes itself, if it would live,
Where little children age before their time,
And life wears down the edges of the mind,
Where the old man sits with mind grown cold,
While bones and sinew, blood and cell, go slowly down to death,
Where fear companions each day's life,
And Perfect Love seems long delayed.
CHRISTMAS IS WAITING TO BE BORN:
In you, in me, in all mankind.

Christmas Is the Season of the Heart

The Time of forgiveness for injuries past,
The Sacrament of sharing without balancing the deed,
The Moment of remembrance of graces forgotten,
The Poem of joy making light the spirit,
The Sense of renewal restoring the soul,
The Day of thanksgiving for the goodness of God.
CHRISTMAS IS THE SEASON OF THE HEART.

Christmas Returns

Christmas returns, as it always does, with its assurance that life is good.
It is the time of lift to the spirit,
　　When the mind feels its way into the commonplace,
　　And senses the wonder of simple things: an evergreen tree,
　　Familiar carols, merry laughter.
It is the time of illumination,
　　When candles burn, and old dreams
　　Find their youth again.
It is the time of pause,
　　When forgotten joys come back to mind, and past
　　dedications renew their claim.
It is the time of harvest for the heart,
　　When faith reaches out to mantle all high endeavor,
　　And love whispers its magic word to everything that breathes.
Christmas returns, as it always does, with its assurance that life is good.

Gifts on My Altar

I place these gifts on my altar this Christmas;
　　Gifts that are mine, as the years are mine.
　　The quiet hopes that flood the earnest cargo of my dreams;
　　The best of all good things for those I love.
　　A fresh new trust for all whose faith is dim.
　　The love of life, God's precious gift in reach of all:
　　Seeing in each day the seeds of the morrow,
　　Finding in each struggle the strength of renewal,
　　Seeking in each person the face of my brother.
I place these gifts on my altar this Christmas;
　　Gifts that are mine, as the years are mine.

The Growing Edge

All around us worlds are dying and new worlds are being born;
    All around us life is dying and life is being born:
        The fruit ripens on the tree;
    The roots are silently at work in the darkness of the earth
Against the time when there shall be new leaves, fresh blossoms,
        green fruit.
        Such is the growing edge!
It is the extra breath from the exhausted lung,
    The one more thing to try when all else has failed,
The upward reach of life when weariness closes in upon all endeavor.
        This is the basis of hope in moments of despair,
        The incentive to carry on when times are out of joint
And men have lost their reason; the source of confidence
    When worlds crash and dreams whiten into ash.
The birth of a child—life's most dramatic answer to death—
    This is the Growing Edge incarnate,
    Look well to the growing edge!

The Work of Christmas

    When the song of the angels is stilled,
    When the star in the sky is gone,
    When the kings and princes are home,
    When the shepherds are back with their flock,
    The work of Christmas begins:
        To find the lost,
        To heal the broken,
        To feed the hungry,
        To release the prisoner,
        To rebuild the nations,
        To bring peace among brothers,
        To make music in the heart.

I Will Sing a New Song

The old song of my spirit has wearied itself out.
It has long ago been learned by heart;
It repeats itself over and over,
Bringing no added joy to my days or lift to my spirit.

I will sing a new song.
I must learn the new song for the new needs.
I must fashion new words born of all the new growth
    of my life—of my mind—of my spirit.
I must prepare for new melodies that have
    never been mine before,
That all that is within me may lift my voice unto God.
Therefore, I shall rejoice with each new day
And delight my spirit in each fresh unfolding.
I will sing, this day, a new song unto the Lord.

Christmas Is the Season of Affirmation

I affirm my faith in the little graces of life:
    The urgency of growth, the strength of laughter, the vitality of
        friendship.
I affirm my confidence in the dignity of man:
    His fortitude in despair, his strength in weakness, his love in hatred.
I affirm my joy in the experience of living:
    The fragrance of nostalgia, the scattered moments of delight, the
        exhilaration of danger.
I affirm my need of my fellows:
    The offerings of faiths, the gifts of variety, the quality of difference.
I affirm my hunger for God:
    The desire for fulfillment, the ache for understanding, the sense
        of peace.
        CHRISTMAS IS MY SEASON OF AFFIRMATION

At Christmastime

The tides flow out from the Inner Sea
At Christmastime:
They find their way to many shores
With gifts of remembrance, thoughts of love—
Though the world be weary and the days afraid
The heart renews its life and the mind takes hope
From the tides that flow from the Inner Sea
At Christmastime.

This Is the Season of Promise

Let the bells be silenced
Let the gifts be stillborn
Let cheer be muted
Let music be soundless
   Violence stalks the land:
   Soaring above the cry of the dying
   Rising above the whimper of the starving
   Floating above the flying machines of death
      Listen to the long stillness:
      New life is stirring
      New dreams are on the wing
      New hopes are being readied:
Mankind is fashioning a new heart
Mankind is forging a new mind
God is at work.

This is the Season of Promise.

The Sacrament of Christmas

I make an act of faith toward all mankind,
  Where doubts would linger and suspicions brood.
I make an act of joy toward all sad hearts,
  Where laughter pales and tears abound.
I make an act of strength toward feeble things,
  Where life grows dim and death draws near.
I make an act of trust toward all of life,
  Where fears preside and distrusts keep watch.
I make an act of love toward friend and foe,
  Where trust is weak and hate burns bright.
I make a deed to God of all my days—
And look out on life with quiet eyes.

The Season of Remembrance

Again and again, it comes:
The Time of Recollection,
The Season of Remembrance.
Empty vessels of hope fill up again;
Forgotten treasures of dreams reclaim
    their place;
Long-lost memories come trooping back to me.
This is my season of remembrance,
My time of recollection.

Into the challenge of my anguish
I throw the strength of all my hope:
I match the darts of my despair
    with the treasures of my dreams;
Upon the current of my heart
I float the burdens of the years;
I challenge the mind of death
    with my love of life.
Such to me is the Time of Recollection,
The season of Remembrance.

Against the Background of the Year

Our Father, another Christmas has moved within our ken and our minds linger over many moments that stand stark against the background of the year—

Moments that filled our cup of fear to the brim, spilling over into the byways of our mind until there was no longer room even to know that we were afraid—

Moments of decision, when all that we were seemed to hang in the balance, waiting for a gentle nudging of Thy spirit to break the tie and send us on with a new direction, a new desire, and new way of life—

Moments of sadness, brought on by the violent collapse or quiet sagging of a lifetime of dream-building upon which our hopes and aspirations rested in sure integrity—

Moments of awareness, when our whole landscape was invaded by the glow of Thy spirit, making dead things come to newness of life and old accepted ways turn into radiant shafts of beauteous light—

Moments of joy mingled with the deadly round of daily living, when all our inward parts clapped their hands and a new song was born in our heart—

Moments of peace amid the noisy clang of many conflicts within and without—

Moments of reassurance, when we discovered that our searching anxieties were groundless, without foundation—

Moments of reconciliation, made possible by a deeper understanding and a greater wisdom—

Moments of renewal, without which life would have been utterly impossible and for us this day there would be no Christmas and no day—

Moments of praise and thanksgiving when, in one grand sweep, the sheer wonder and beauty of living overwhelmed us—

Our Father, another Christmas has moved into our ken and our minds linger over many moments that stand stark against the background of the year.

Life Seems Unaware

Once again the smell of death rides on the winds
    And fear lurks within the shadows of the mind.
One by one the moments tick away.
    Days and nights are interludes
Between despairing hope and groping faith.
    Of this bleak desolation, Life seems unaware:
Seeds still die and live again in answer to their kind;
    Fledgling birds awake to life from prison house of shell;
Flowers bloom and blossoms fall as harbingers of fruit to come;
    The newborn child comes even on the wings of death;
The thoughts of men are blanketed by dreams
    Of tranquil days and peaceful years,
When love unfettered will keep the heart and mind
    In ways of life that crown our days with light.

Christmas Meditations

There must always be provision for the ample moment when an event takes on the character of the Sacramental, however such an event may be named in the calendar. The true significance of the event is to be found in the quality of celebration which it inspires in the heart.

A Moment Is *the* Moment

PART I

Again and again in the course of the history of nations and individuals, a single event becomes the critical point by which the life or death of vast issues is determined. It is impossible to know of what any event is prophetic and how many strands of destiny are caught in a single pattern that is woven before our very eyes. A chance word overheard by a passerby may alter the entire structure of his subsequent days. An impression made upon the mind of a growing child by some nameless person who crossed his path and disappeared may be the motif that shapes the fate of millions of people years after, when the child has become a leader of men strategically placed at a fateful crossroads in the history of a people.

It is impossible to know when a moment is *the* moment, when an act is *the* act, when an issue is *the* issue. In 165 B.C. a Jewish leader, Judas Maccabeus, with or without a sense of destiny, spearheaded the funded hopes and dreams and dedicated passions of Israel and flung them triumphantly in the face of the legions of Antiochus Epiphanes, in a decisive battle that unraveled a thread out of which the patterns of Christianity and Mohammedanism were woven. It is well within the mark to say that if Judas Maccabeus had been defeated, it is not unreasonable to assume that Judaism would have perished; and without Judaism there would have been no Christianity and no Mohammedanism. The human family would have been easily involved indefinitely in pouring out its votive offerings before altars of idolatry, stark and meaningless, yielding no hope and no response.

It is in celebration of this event, of what may be regarded as unconscious destiny, that the Feast of Lights is commemorated for eight days in December in countless Jewish homes all over the world. A single event in history, a man who refuses to renounce his faith either by default or defeat becomes, in the circling wisdom of a Providence rich in variety and creativity, the gate through which have marched hundreds of generations of men to a life abundant and a hope undimmed.

A Moment Is *the* Moment
PART II

There must always remain in every people's life some space for the celebration of those events of the past that bear their fruit in the present. Those events in which the race seems to catch its breath and to give the long look forward and backward. Such events are surrounded by a quality all their own—and yet they seem to gather into themselves the essence of all striving and the meaning of all hope.

Chanukah is such an event. Here was a moment in the life of Israel in which a people was faced with an ultimate choice: On the one hand, to renounce the very heart of a faith in one God with whom they were covenanted and to give a false value to a profound communal commitment. On the other hand, to say "Yes" to a truth by which the steps of the past had been guided when there was no light, and no guide save one. One man in his vision became, first, a whole nation and then the whole race of mankind, as he affirmed in his deed—the Lord God is one and alone is worthy to be worshiped and to be praised. In steady stream there has flowed from him a way that, for generations of men, has become The Way.

Christmas is such an event. Here was a moment in the life of Israel in which a baby was born, in surroundings as commonplace as the leaves and branches of the olive tree. In him was seen, by many, that for which their hearts had hungered and of which their dreams had foretold. He grew into manhood, exhibiting in word and deed a fresh new quality of the age-old response of the spirit of man to the call of God. God was everything to him. His was the vision of a great creative ideal that all men are children of God, that the normal relation of one man to another is love (anything else is against life), and that there is a personal Power, God, equally available to rich and poor, to Jew and Gentile, to men and women, to the wise and the foolish, to the just and the unjust.

For millions his birth marks the turning point in human history, and Christmas is the event above all events. For it marks the moment when a new meaning is given to ancient words: The eyes of the blind are opened, the captives are set free, and the acceptable year of the Lord is become literal truth!

Chanukah and Christmas spring from the same womb and are mothered by the same brooding spirit. One marks freedom from tyranny and the preservation of the eternal Light for all the generations of men. The other announces that there is a Presence in the common life, a Light that lighteth every man that cometh into the world.

"But Then Face to Face"

For now we see through a glass, darkly; but then face to face. . . .

It is the judgment scene.
The climax of man's life has come at last;
The oriental despot sits enthroned.
Before him come the peoples of the earth.
Here are no men, no women, boys or girls
Struggling for rank, wealth, class, or power.
No race or tribe has standing here.
All walls that separate, divide,
By the moving drama are pushed aside.
Each life is freed of all pretense,

Each shadowy seeming swept away
By the mighty spread of ceaseless light.
    "I was sick, comfortless;
    I was hungry, desperate;
    I was lonely, wretched;
    I was in prison, forsaken . . ."
Strange awful words from Him;
Words more searching followed after:
    "I know your tasks were manifold;
    Unyielding claims consumed your thoughts.
    There was no time to be at ease with deeds,
    To give yourself beyond your creed.
    Oh, I know about your temperament, your health,
    Somehow you could not manage all your chores,
    Excuses came to reinforce the empty feeling of your heart.
    I know how hard it was for you.
    You did not want to be an easy touch!
    Beyond all else, your ties of blood;
    Charity must begin at home.
Besides,
    You did not know, but are you sure?
    Do you recall the flashes of concern
    That held you in your place that day?
    I see you do remember well.
    Again they came and then again,
    Until at last they came no more;
    Only the hollow darkness of the self cut off
    From all the pain and pathos of the world.
    No word of mine can alter what your days have done."
The story of your life is what the judge reveals.
From the relentless judgment, is there no appeal?

The Gift of Grace

This is the season of Christmas. For many people, in many places, it is a time of great pressure and activity, a time when nerves are tense, and when a great deal of anxiety hovers over the common life. And this is just the reversal of what the mood and the meaning of Christmas really are. I would like to suggest, then, that for those of you who care deeply about the meaning of your own lives and the significance of moments of high celebration, that you would do two things during this season. One, that you will seek reconciliation with any person or persons with whom you have, at the moment, a ruptured or unhappy relationship. During the year that is rapidly coming to a close, you have perhaps had many experiences with many kinds of people, those with whom you live, those with whom you work, or those with whom you play, and in the course of these goings-on there have been times when the relationships heightened and were thrown out of joint, and a desert and a sea developed between you and someone else. And you were so busy with your own responsibilities, and perhaps so full of hostility yourselves, that there was no time to give to the business and the experience and the grace of reconciliation. So will you think about such a person, find a way by which you can restore a lost harmony, so that your Christmas gift to yourselves will be peace between you and someone else.

The second is just as simple. Will you with your imagination, with your fancy, will you conjure up into your minds a gift of grace that you might give to someone for whom you have no obligation, someone whose need is not so great that if you don't respond to it during this season you will feel guilty—but someone upon whom you might confer a private blessing. It may be just to pick up the telephone and call someone whose life is not tied to yours in any way, but someone about whom you know something and with this knowledge as a background you say a word of reassurance, of comfort, of delight, of satisfaction—so that you will feel that out of the fullness of your own hearts, you have conferred upon some unsuspecting human being a gentle grace that makes the season a good and whole and hale and happy time.

The Seasons of God

In one of the letters of Fénelon he writes:

Time bears a very different aspect at different seasons of one's life, but there is one maxim which applies equally to all seasons, namely, that none should go by uselessly; that every season carries with it various duties of God's own appointing, and concerning the discharge of which we must give account to Him, since from the first to the last moment of life God never means us to look upon any time as purposeless, either to be used as our own apart from Him, or lost. The important thing is to know how He would have us use it, and this is to be learned not by an eager and uneasy ardor, which is much more calculated to confuse than to enlighten us concerning our duties, but by pure and upright heart, seeking God in simplicity and diligence in receiving all of experiences which He would provide for us, for remember we lose time not only by doing nothing, or doing amiss, but also by doing things in themselves right, which things yet are not what God would have us do. Our general rule for the right use of time is to accustom yourself to live in continual dependence upon the Spirit of God, receiving whatever He vouchsafes to give from one moment to another.

Those are ancient words, written many years ago, addressed to a particular time and condition, which time and condition may seem to be limited to a particular moment in human history, but the insight at work is of profound significance. It says that time has an aspect which is always a reflection of the particular season obtaining in the individual life.

When you were a little boy or a little girl, time meant certain things to you that it did not mean as you grew older. When I was a boy, time was very fluid until Thanksgiving, but from Thanksgiving to December 24, time had a very crucial significance. Every moment of every waking hour had to count toward a particular event which was significant in my life: the coming of Christmas and Christmas presents. I had a feeling that there was some relationship between the presents I would get on Christmas morning and the character of my behavior from Thanksgiving until Christmas Eve; hence the event of my life made the time interval which was lived under the shadow of that event very, very significant.

Because time has this dimension of relativity for us, we are apt to miss one of the important revelations which time, in my judgment, expresses about the meaning of the purposes of life and what may be called the work of the seasons of God. Just as there are seasons in nature and seasons in the life of an individual, seasons which are broken up in terms of babyhood, childhood, youth, maturity, and old age, on a wider canvas, an almost timeless canvas, God has seasons. In His seasons, His plans and dreams and purposes become operative, are set in motion. Therefore, the living of the private life is related to the seasons the individual is experiencing as he moves from infancy to old age, and these are related to the seasons of nature.

They are also involved in the seasons of a nation as it goes through certain experiences. As it grows in years and the quality of its experiences thickens and deepens, another dimension comes over its life. Nations, too, come to a period of old age, of decline and death.

Behind all of these, or beyond all of these, I think there are vast creative intents, which must be in the mind of the Creator: the building of a world, the making of the earth in the light of the other planets. In turn, these planets relate to other planets, one solar system relates to another system, ad infinitum. Creative and intimate harmony and order run through the whole process.

Where I live my little segment of time, I must live it in the light of the fact that all of the vast complex of which my little segment is a part, gives to my little segment its meaning. Therefore, I cannot say about my life that it is of no account, I cannot say of the time that I am living that nothing seems to be happening, because this is not one of the great and tempestuous or creative moments in human history or in the history of worlds. My time is my time, and I must live my time with as much fullness and significance as I am capable of, because my little segment of time is all the time that I have. I cannot wait to begin living meaningfully when I will have more time, because all the time that I can ever experience is the time interval of my moment, so that my minutes, my hours, my days, my months, must be full of my flavor and my meaning.

Therefore, I will bring to my day, as commonplace and insignificant as it may seem, the fullest mind, the greatest purpose, and the most significant intent of which I am capable, because my time is not merely mine, but because my time is in His hands as well.

The Good Deed

What happens when you do a good deed that meets some urgent need in the life of another person? Do you share with the person anything beyond the deed that is done, beyond the gift that is given?

Does the other person share with you anything beyond the deed that is accepted, beyond the gift that is received? Suppose the deed done and the gift given were the outward expression of an inward urge? Suppose the necessity to give were an inner necessity, generated by the discovery within yourself that your life is marked off from another life by the thinnest lines?

It is a world-shattering disclosure that the stream of life is a single stream, though it takes various forms as it spills over into time and space. This disclosure is made to anyone whose discipline sends him on high adventure within his own spirit, his own inner life. By prayer, by the deep inward gaze which opens the eyes of the soul to behold the presence of God, a man feels the steady rhythm of life itself. He seems to be behind the scene of all persons, things, and events. The deep hunger to be understood is at last seen to be one and the same with the hunger to understand.

Out of such an experience a new perspective emerges. Consciously now, the primary function or mission of life becomes that of achieving in act what one has experienced in insight. One is ever on the hunt for openings in others through which this may be achieved. Human need in all of its dimensions is the swinging door into the innermost life of another. To put it differently, it is the point at which the spirit is most highly sensitized for communication.

If a man is moved from within his own spirit to do the deed of ministering to the need of another, and if the need of another is the point at which the spirit is most highly sensitized to communication, then it follows that the good deed is a meeting place for the mingling of one life with another. What a man has experienced in insight he achieves in the deed. What a difference giving makes now. It is no longer an offering merely of money or time or services, viewed as a sacrifice or a cause for merit, recognition, or glory. It is a simple sacrament, involving all of a person as his spirit moves through the swinging door of need into the very citadel of another's spirit.

To Share the Best

No man can escape the urgency to share as an offering of his heart that which to him has the deepest meaning. Often there is the pretension that this is not so. For there seems to be present in the human spirit a desire to cover up, to hide for safekeeping the most precious thing, the most valuable possession. The decisive quest is to find someone worthy to receive the offering or some altar upon which it may be laid. You have seen the little boy go through the treasures in his pocket—a string, piece of colored glass, a coin, a big rubber band, and so forth—to find the one thing that means the most to him—to offer as the ultimate test of his devotion or the final tribute to his daring. How many times have you gone through your treasure chest to find something that you prize most highly, which thing you wanted to share with someone else as the ultimate expression of the quality of your caring?

Little by little a new element begins to emerge—there appears the desire to know what the other person prizes as of most value and to seek to make that as the offering of the heart. If one does not possess it, then one seeks to find it—if it is a quality, one seeks to develop it; if it is a taste in dress or food, one seeks to acquire it. Such response to another becomes destructive, however, when it means that one person is stretched out of shape in an effort to make to another the most precious offering, to give freely one's choicest possession.

It is one of the great insights of religion that only God is worthy of the best in one's treasure house and the best in one's treasure house is not worthy of Him. The urge to share as an offering of the heart that which has deepest meaning is at bottom the hunger for God. It is deep calling unto deep. Offerings may be made to other human beings in and for themselves and for one's self. But such offerings do not satisfy, nor do they bring peace to the spirit. It is only when the offering is seen as being made to the Highest, to God, however crude may be the altar upon which it rests, is the deep need in us all satisfied and our spirits come into the great Peace.

Awareness of Another's Need

One of the oldest and least known of the Negro spirituals is this:

> I don't want nobody's bloodstains on my hands.
> I don't want nobody's bloodstains on my hands.
> I'm going to work, fight and pray,
> And live more holy every day.
> I don't want nobody's bloodstains on my hands.

The idea which it embodies is echoed in the familiar poem of Edna St. Vincent Millay: "I shall die but that is all that I shall do for Death. . . . Am I a spy in the land of the living, that I should deliver men to Death?"*

To live without doing violence to another human being in the living! This is a task difficult and searching. Often our knowledge of other people's needs is so limited that it is altogether possible for us to do violence to them without ever knowing it. There is no cry more pathetic than "If I had only known" or "There was no way for me to know." We are all involved in that kind of violence.

Sometimes we do violence because of thoughtlessness. In the intense concentration upon our own selves, our own needs, our own desires, we dull the edges of our sensitiveness to the needs and the desires of others. Ultimately, we find ourselves developing a dimness of soul except where the imperious demands of our own egos are at stake. A child can become so concerned with his own life, the demands growing out of his own necessities, that parents become means to ends in which they do not share. It is a very shocking discovery sometimes for a son or a daughter to realize that a mother or a father is a human being with problems and needs that are always held in the background before the onrush of a kind of adolescent insistence. Sometimes a parent becomes so engrossed in the complexities of his personal life, the rigors of work, the involvements of profession that he is apt to be unmindful of the hunger of the heart of his child. Yes, we do violence to others through thoughtlessness.

But none of the above deals with the crucial issue raised by the song. Here we are faced with the kind of violence that is deliberate.

---

* From "The Conscientious Objector."

There are times when to save our own skins, we offer someone else up for sacrifice. There are times when through cowardice, fear, or hostility, we refrain from doing the thing that would rescue another person from the clutches of disaster. The temptation is always on the side of retaliation, of self-preservation, even if it means leading death in some form to the other person's door. These early singers suggested that there is but one way by which the human spirit may be protected from the fearful jeopardy and that is by living "holy every day." This can only be achieved by working, struggling, and praying, to the end that the great energies of God might be realized through one's whole life, rendering him more and more immune to the tendency to do violence to another, even on behalf of oneself.

The Point of Greatest Need

I was standing on the corner waiting for a streetcar when I noticed a man seated behind the steering wheel of an automobile parked on the opposite side of the street. He was busily engaged in making notes in a little book. Presently he put his book away, started the motor, and then looked over in my direction with a broad, inviting smile on his face. I smiled in return, thinking at once that in some way our paths had crossed. He opened the door of the car, called to me, extending an invitation to ride downtown if I were going in that direction.

As we rode along, I listened for some word in the conversation that would reveal his identity or the fact that, at some time in the past, we had met. It was soon clear that we were total strangers but that out of the graciousness of his heart he had offered me a lift. He was a salesman, speaking with a broken accent, who was glad of the chance to share what he had with someone whose need was specific at the point of his fullness. I was reminded of a very precious friend who has the habit of stopping at a certain corner each morning, offering a ride to any person who may be standing there waiting for the bus to go uptown. According to the testimony of this friend, each morning was a heightened adventure in understanding a new person, a different person. A rare richness has accrued to her because of the cross-fertilization of so many different human beings with whom she has shared a practical fullness at the point of a practical and felt, immediate need.

Perhaps there is nothing more exhilarating to the spirit than to be able to minister to the needs of others at the time when a particular need is most acutely felt. This is the essence of the spirit of Christmas. We spend much time and energy during this season of the year in selecting gifts to be given to our friends. Very often these gifts are shared with the desire that they will make the right kind of impression on the receiver; sometimes the impression that we seek to make is in terms of our abundance, or our discriminating taste, or our hope for something of like kind in return.

Very rarely indeed is our giving out of the fullness of our possessions at the point of our friend's greatest felt need. The result is that Christmas means fatigue, exhaustion, a kind of world weariness that makes for self-pity. It must be borne in mind that true friends are those who accept us as we are, for what we are in ourselves. Their affection and their understanding cannot be purchased by gifts. A thoughtful telephone call on Christmas Eve or Christmas Day, a hand-written note of intimate recollections, will often lift up and strengthen the heart of another, leaving a long, sustaining afterglow when a gift, however costly, will only be a gift.

The true meaning of Christmas is expressed in the sharing of one's graces in a world in which it is so easy to become calloused, insensitive, and hard. Once this spirit becomes a part of man's life, every day is Christmas, and every night is freighted with anticipations of the dawning of fresh, and perhaps holy, adventure.

A Unique Christmas Story

"It is a long story," said my friend on a Christmas morning more than forty years ago. "My earliest memories were of the sea and the freighter that had been my home for so long a time. It was an American ship whose captain came from New England.

"As we entered the Gulf of Mexico the captain lay dying. He called me to his bedside and put into my hand a somewhat faded envelope containing my vital statistics. I was born in Calcutta but was kidnaped at a very early age to be a companion to the captain's son who was about my age. The sea was the only life that I had known.

"I entered the country at a Texas port and was soon on my own with some money to sustain me until I could find work. One day when I was at the railway station looking at a private railway car unlike anything that I had ever seen, a man came down the steps, engaged me in conversation which ended with my being offered a job. As a part of the arrangement I was given living quarters in the basement of his home.

"A few days after my first Christmas on shore I noticed a small group of street urchins quarreling over the faded tinsel on the discarded Christmas tree that the family had thrown into the alley. A great inspiration came to me. On the spot I made a resolution to *do* something about it.

"By the time the next Christmas season came, I put my plan into action. I found a group of children who would have little, if any, Christmas joy. After much care I came to know them personally and to secure the name of one toy that each child would like to have. These toys were purchased, carefully wrapped, and labeled with each child's name. In addition, there were small bags of candy, nuts, and fruit.

"The family with whom I lived permitted me to bring the children to my quarters for Christmas morning. It was all very simple—a decorated tree, packages of gayly wrapped presents, and bags of nuts, fruit, and candy. They sang Christmas carols, there was a little prayer, and the gifts were distributed. My family was invited downstairs to be a part of what was happening. They were so moved that for the rest of my time there I was urged to have my Christmas party in their living room upstairs.

"When I moved to this little town in Ohio some twenty years ago, I repeated my Texas experience. Early in the fall I visit all of the children or sometimes they come to see me. I find out from each child the one toy or gift he or she wants for Christmas. Fortunately I have the cooperation of the manager in a very large department store in the neighboring city where I work. The gifts are bought, wrapped, and the name of each child put on his or her package. This in addition to the nuts, candy, and fruit.

"There were two adults here this morning who were children around my tree many years ago. It is a satisfying feeling and it gives me something which was denied me in my own childhood."

In His Image

Many years ago a brilliant young sociologist at Columbia College delivered a lecture to his class on "The Philosophy of a Fool." He ended the first part of his address with these words: "On the seventh day, therefore, God could not rest. In the morning and the evening He busied Himself with terrible and beautiful concoctions and in the twilight of the seventh day He finished that which is of more import than the beasts of the earth and the fish of the sea and the lights of the firmament. And he called it Imagination because it was made in His own image; and those unto whom it is given shall see God."

We are accustomed to thinking of the imagination as a useful tool in the hands of the artist as he reproduces in varied forms that which he sees beyond the rim of fact that encircles him. There are times when the imagination is regarded as a delightful and often whimsical characteristic of what we are pleased to call "the childish mind." Our judgment trembles on the edge of condescension, pity, or even ridicule when imagination is confused with fancy in the reports that are given of the inner workings of the mind of "the simpleton" or "the fool." We recognize and applaud the bold and audacious leap of the mind of the scientist when it soars far out beyond that which is known and established, to fix a beachhead on distant, unexplored shores.

But the place where the imagination shows its greatest powers as the *angelos* of God is in the miracle which it creates when one man, standing in his place, is able, while remaining there, to put himself in another man's place. To send his imagination forth to establish a beachhead in another man's spirit, and from that vantage point so to blend with the other's landscape that what he sees and feels is authentic—this is the great adventure in human relations. But this is not enough. The imagination must report its findings accurately without regard to all prejudgments and private or collective fears. But this is not enough. There must be both a spontaneous and a calculating response to such knowledge which will result in sharing of resources at their deepest level.

Very glibly are we apt to use such words as "sympathy," "companion," "sitting where they sit," but to experience their meaning is to be rocked to one's foundations. The simple truth is, we resist making room for considerations that swerve us out of the path of preoccupation with ourselves, our needs, our problems. We make our imagination a thing of corruption when we give it range only over our own affairs. Here we experience the magnification of our own ills, the distortion of our own problems, and the enlargement of the areas of our misery. What we do not permit our imagination to do in the work of understanding others, turns in upon ourselves with disaster and sometimes terror.

To be to another human being what is needed at the time that the need is most urgent and most acutely felt—this is to participate in the precise act of redemption. The imagination acting under the most stringent orders can develop a technique all its own in locating and reporting to us its findings. We are not the other persons, we are ourselves. All that they are experiencing we can never know—but we can make accurate soundings, which, when properly read, will enable us to be to them what we could never be without such awareness. The degree to which our imagination becomes the *angelos* of God, we ourselves may become *His instruments*.

Grace at Meat

To be alive is to participate responsibly in the experiences of life. Men say grace at meat not only because they feel a sense of gratitude to God for sustaining providence, but also out of a deep sense of responsibility to the life that has been yielded so that they may be sustained for one more day. The bacon that a man ate for breakfast, at some moment in the past, was alive with vibrant, elemental health and vigor. Who can measure the reaches of aliveness of a hog, wallowing in murky contentment in the summer sun? To what subtle overtones of aliveness is he responding in the guttural overflow from his drooling mouth? There comes a day when he must die— "be slaughtered" is the acrid word we use. What are the paroxysms of lightning intimations of meanings that thud through his body at the first fall of the bludgeon? In utter accuracy, he dies that we may live.

Thus, as we partake of his body, we pause, like the stillness of absolute motion, to salute his leave-taking of life. Because of what he yielded and because of the myriad yieldings of many forms of life, we are able to live and carry on. This means that our life is not our own.

Every minute of life we are faced with the relentless urgency to make good in our own lives for the lives that are lost for us. Quite consciously, then, I see my responsibility to all that has gone into the making of me—not only in terms of food but also in terms of the total contribution that has been made to my life both by the past and the present. I must live my life responsibly or lose my right to self-respect and to integrity.

This basic fact has profound bearing on the notion of freedom. Freedom means the possession of a sense of alternatives. It does not mean the absence of responsibility, but it does mean a sense of alternatives with reference to the experiences of life. If it be true, as we have pointed out, that to be alive is to be under active obligation to many other units of life, then the measure of my freedom is the measure of my responsibility. If I can do as I please without any sense of responsibility, then my alternatives are zero. I *must* select, *must* choose the option which will make possible the largest fulfillment of my own life plus the other lives of which I am the shared expression. One option is always available to me: I can choose the things for which I shall stand and work and live, and the things *against* which I shall stand and work and live. To yield this right is to fail utterly my own self and all others upon whom I must depend. The highest role of freedom is the choice of the kind of option that will make of my life not only a benediction breathing peace but also a vital force of redemption to all I touch. This would mean, therefore, that wherever I am, *there* the very Kingdom of God is at hand.

Our Father, may our lives fulfill in themselves the hopes and unfulfilled yearnings of all whose stirrings for wholeness and completion are dim and inarticulate because of the burden of hate, weariness, and misery under which their days are cast. May we achieve the freedom of sons of God, for whom every day is a Day of Judgment and every act a sacrament of thy Presence and every purpose a fresh channel through which thy Love pours forth its healing to the children of men.

The Self-giving Impulse

One of the great gifts of God to man is the sense of concern that one individual may develop for another, the impulse toward self-giving that finds its ultimate fulfillment in laying down one's life for his friend. It is difficult to keep the sense of concern free from those subtle desires to place another under obligation, and thereby stifle and strangle that which one wishes to bless and heal.

When I ask myself why I try to help others, what reply do I get? Is it merely an effort on my part to build up my own sense of significance? Am I trying to prove my own superiority? When I do something for another which involves a clear definitive act of concern on my part, do I spoil it by saying to myself or to another, "Look what I did for him. And now he treats me as he does"? Or do we say, "After all I have done for him, he should do anything I ask of him"?

Is our sense of concern used as a means for gaining power over others? To be able to give oneself without expecting to be paid back, to love disinterestedly but with warmth and understanding, is to be spiritually mature and godlike and to lay hold on the most precious possessions vouchsafed to the human race.

The Art of Grace

Again and again we are impressed with the fact that little things can make big differences. A little act of kindness at a moment of great need makes all the difference between sunshine and shadows. A smile at the right moment may make an intolerable burden lighter. Just a note bearing a message of simple interest or concern or affection may give to another the radically needed assurance. A simple "Thank you" has softened many a hard situation or punctured the crust of many a "hardboiled" person.

There is always a place for the graceful gesture, the thoughtful remark, the sensitive response. It is what may be called "living flexibly."

There is often confusion between formality and ungraciousness, or informality and graciousness. One may be gracious without fawning and affectation. There is no greater compliment to be given than to say: "You are very kind. To know you is to make life itself a more satisfying experience." This means that such a person has learned, or developed, or been born with, the fine art of gracious living. It is the antidote to much of the crudeness and coarseness of modern life.

Our reputation for bad manners and for rudeness is unenviable. The derogatory names that we use to tag other peoples and other races, the supercilious flippancy used as the common coin of daily intercourse, all these things reflect a carelessness in living that hurts and bruises, often where there is no intent to injure and destroy. It is true that little things often make big differences.

The Gift of Memory

What a priceless gift is memory! Suppose you had no memory, how difficult life would be; every day, and every minute in the day, you would have to begin everything for the first time. Learning would be impossible and education would be meaningless. We have the amazing power to carry along with us, moment by moment, a vast accumulation of things done, of experiences lived through, of skills and techniques that have long since been learned by heart and put aside to be brought promptly into play on demand.

It is in order to raise the question as to the use that is made of memory. How do you use it? There are some people who use their memories to store away all the unpleasant things they experience. Every slight they have received from the hands of another is neatly labeled with the offender's name and put away as in a card catalogue. When some later contact with the person is made, they run through their files, lift out the old offense, and dress it up to be paraded in the new encounter. The habit grows, until at last their storehouse is full of unpleasant things which send their poisonous fumes all through the corridors of the mind, filling them with suspicion, resentment, and hate.

There are others who use their memories to store away the pleasant things of experience. Such memories become a vast storehouse to which, at a minute's notice, they turn to restore their faith and reestablish their confidence in life at difficult and trying times. The next time you feel that life is mean or completely evil and that there is no good in it for you or anyone else, try this: make a list of some of the beautiful things you have seen, the breathlessly kind things people have done for you without obligation, the gracious moments that have turned up in the week's encounters.

Memory is one of God's great gifts to the human spirit without which neither life nor experience could have any meaning. Moreover, without it we could not be *human* beings.

The Gift of Imagination

One of the most positive expressions of the life of God in the life of man is the gift of imagination. If it were not for the imagination, reflective thinking would be quite impossible. Memory would be mere physical sensation that had left its traces in the nervous system. It is unlikely, even, that human speech would have developed at all. Think of it: because of the gift of imagination, you can go back into the past, relive experiences that are no longer present, leap into the future, anticipate that which is yet to come, walk through a wall, or span an ocean in the twinkling of an eye.

Perhaps most important of all, without imagination human love would be impossible of achievement for there can be no love among human beings where there is no power of self-projection. The mechanism of love is the ability to put oneself in the life of another and to look out upon the world through the other's eyes—to enter into the feeling and thinking and reacting of another, even as one remains oneself. This can never be done completely; hence the element of profound frustration and tragedy at the center of the love experience.

Imagination is the creative vehicle that carries one spirit into the dwelling place of another. There could be no sympathy in the world if men had not the gift of imagination. The spirit of man could never take flight in dreams, hopes, or aspirations if there were no wings of imagination given as a part of man's equipment for life. Man would merely be his little self—no more, no less. There could be no hope for anything beyond. Think of it, just to be myself, myself alone, knowing forever that nothing could ever happen to me that would go beyond my present self!

The witness of God's spirit in man's spirit is symbolized by imagination, without which there could be no sense of sin, no repentance and contrition, no tenderness and sympathy, no love and no hope.

Life, an Offering to God

Many, many years ago, a Hindu poet wrote:

> Love not the world nor yet forsake
> Its gifts in fear and hate.
> Thy life to God an offering make,
> And to Him dedicate.

We are all involved in life in its varied aspects and responsibilities. The daily routine carries its own toll of energies and processes. The struggle for bread and shelter continues to the very end to beat at our lives and our very spirits with an insistence that cannot be ignored. For many there are additional cares that go beyond the demands of our own personal survival and encompass the tender threads of the lives of others to whom we are bound by ties of blood and birth.

Beyond all this, there are areas of the common life in which we must do our part in order that the very fabric of society may be maintained against collapse and disintegration. There are dreams, hopes, and yearnings which possess our lives, calling us away from the usual round and the common tasks. In the midst of all these pressures and many more, life for us becomes entangled or again and again bogs down.

There comes a moment when we are in utter revolt—something deep within us becomes tired, weary, exhausted, and finally, outraged. What we long for in deep anxiety is some haven, some place of retreat, some time of quiet where our bruised and shredded spirits may find healing and restoration. One form that this anxiety takes is to hate life and to fear tomorrow. For such the ancient poet speaks a timely word. All such experiences are a part of our experience and must be regarded as life's gifts. Whatever may be the uniqueness of a man's experience, he must remember that nothing that is happening to him is separated from that which is common to man.

The answer to all of this reaction of deep anxiety and anguish is, says the poet: "Thy life to God an offering make, and to Him dedicate." And the meaning of this? If I make of my life an offering and a dedication to God, then this dedication will include all of my entanglements and involvements. There follows, then, a radical change over my entire landscape and miraculously I am free at my center.

It is for this reason that it is well, again and again, to reestablish my dedication, to make repeatedly an offering of my life. I must keep my dedication up to date with my experiencing.

The Desert Dweller

He has lived in the desert so long that all of its moods have long since become a part of the daily rhythm of his life. But it is not that fact that is of crucial importance. For many years it has been his custom to leave a lighted lantern by the roadside at night to cheer the weary traveler. Beside the lantern there is a note which gives detailed directions as to where his cottage may be found so that if there is distress or need, the stranger may find help. It is a very simple gesture full of beauty and wholeness. To him it is not important who the stranger may be, it is not important how many people pass in the night and go on their way. The important thing is that the lantern burns every night and every night the note is there, "just in case."

Years ago, walking along a road outside Rangoon, I noted at intervals along the way a roadside stone with a crock of water and, occasionally, some fruit. Water and fruit were put there by Buddhist priests to comfort and bless any passerby—one's spiritual salutation to another. The fact that I was a traveler from another part of the world, speaking a strange language and practicing a different faith, made no difference. What mattered was the fact that I was walking along the road—what my mission was, who I was—all irrelevant.

In your own way, do you keep a lantern burning by the roadside with a note saying where you may be found, "just in case"? Do you place a jar of cool water and a bit of fruit under a tree at the road's turning, to help the needy traveler? God knows the answer and so do you!

Given Element in Life

There is a given element in life. The moment when life becomes life is no man's secret. The moment when life becomes life can never be known. All around us we see evidences of life-movement, forms, structures, in combination, in context. Within ourselves we feel life, it *is* already. Wrapped within it, there seems to be a vast energy without beginning and without end. There is a given element in life.

What is it? All that is ours to know is that life itself is alive. To experience this is to live; it is to feel pulsing through the body energy, vitality, power. It is to feel the lift of the mind to heights of understanding and clarity. It is to walk in the strength of faith restored and a dream that has come to life. It is to continue to give when there is no more to give. It is to hold fast, sometimes against all evidence and all odds. It is to lose everything and yet remain secure against all disaster.

I have wondered about this strange quality of renewal that is one with life itself. May not the clue be nurtured in the fact that life feeds on itself? The grain of corn dies in the earth that the germ hidden away in its core may live, multiply, and bear fruit. All the bloody carnarge surrounding the sustaining of life is grounded in the shrieks and cries of the dying as life consumes itself. Life lives on life; this is the way of life. Here may be found the key to the meaning of all sacrifice and the answer to the urge present in every human heart to *give* itself away.

It is only when the mind is furthest removed from its experience of life that death becomes a separate thing. "He that believeth . . . shall never die" is no empty phrase of Christian piety. It is rather a recognition of eternal process inherent in the experience of life itself. Despite the universal character of the fact, the experience itself is always private, always personal. The *shadow* of death of which the Psalmist speaks is the thing that strikes the terror, the resounding echo of which leaves no ear unassailed. But death itself has no such power because the experience of life contains the fact of death. There is a given element in life—it is the givenness of God. To know this thoroughly is to rob death of its terror and life of its fear.

The Binding Unity

There is a unity that binds all living things into a single whole. This unity is sensed in many ways. Sometimes, when walking alone in the woods far from all the traffic which makes up the daily experience, the stillness settles in the mind. Nothing stirs. The imprisoned self seems to slip outside its boundaries and the ebb and flow of life is keenly felt. One becomes an indistinguishable part of a single rhythm, a single pulse.

Sometimes there is a moment of complete and utter identity with the pain of a loved one; all the intensity and anguish are *felt*. One enters through a single door of suffering into the misery of the whole human race, with no margin left to mark the place which was one's own. What is felt belongs nowhere but is everywhere, binding and holding in a tight circle of agony, until all of life is gathered into a single timeless grasp!

There are other moments when one becomes aware of the thrust of a tingling joy that rises deep within until it bursts forth in radiating happiness that bathes all of life in its glory and its warmth. Pain, sorrow, grief, are seen as joy "becoming" and life gives a vote of confidence to itself, defining its meaning with a sureness that shatters every doubt concerning the broad, free purpose of its goodness.

There are times of personal encounter when a knowledge of caring binds two together and what is felt is good! There is nothing new nor old, only the knowledge that what comes as the flooding insight of love binds all living things into a single whole. The felt reverence spreads and deepens, until to live and to love are to do *one* thing. To hate is to desire the nonexistence of the object of hate. To love is the act of adoration and praise shared with the Creator of life as the Be-all and the End-all of everything that is.

And yet there always remains the hard core of the self, blending and withdrawing, giving and pulling back, accepting and rejoicing, yielding and unyielding—what may this be but the pulsing of the unity that binds all living things in a single whole—the God of life extending Himself in the manifold glories of His creation?

The Strange Irony

There is a strange irony in the usual salutation, "Merry Christmas," when most of the people on this planet are thrown back upon themselves for food which they do not possess, for resources that have long since been exhausted, and for vitality which has already run its course. Despite this fact, Christmas symbolizes hope even at a moment when hope seems utterly fantastic. The raw materials of the Christmas mood are a newborn baby, a family, friendly animals, and labor.

An endless process of births is the perpetual answer of life to the fact of death. It says that life keeps coming on, keeps seeking to fulfill itself, keeps affirming the margin of hope in the presence of desolation, pestilence, and despair. It is not an accident that the birth rate seems always to increase during times of war, when the formal processes of man are engaged in the destructions of others. Welling up out of the depths of vast vitality, there is something at work that is more authentic than the formal discursive design of the human mind. As long as this is true ultimately, despair about the human race is groundless.

The Idiom of Brotherhood

Millions of words have been written and spoken about the meaning of brotherhood in the world. Even the most careful observation reveals that there is something that misses fire, that is essentially inadequate in the usual brotherhood approach to human relations. Of course it is easy to say that the difficulty is in the fact that men who talk glibly about brotherhood are hypocrites and pretenders. Such judgments are apt to be superficial and needlessly cynical. It may be even safe to say that the purveyors of brotherhood are honest, sincere, genuine, and devout.

Nevertheless, the fact remains that even within organizations or institutions essentially built upon the brotherhood notion, the climate in which the individuals function, within and without, is decidedly unbrotherly. The difficulty seems to be in the fact that the concept of brotherhood is regarded as an essentially external relationship between human beings. It is therefore mechanical in character and is concerned with the externals of human behavior.

The conventional approach to the meaning of brotherhood is comparable to the speech of the orator who places his emotions on the outside of the words that he uses and gives the general effect of being phonographic and mechanical. He reminds one of a record that is being played. The approach to the experience of brotherhood should be from the point of view of origin rather than from the point of view of the external relationships between a series of individuals.

It is for this reason that religion approaches the question of brotherhood from the assumption that God is the common father of mankind. The center of focus is on the unity of life guaranteed by the identity of source. The thing that is propelling and mandatory in the practice of brotherhood is deep within the individual human being, and is not conditioned by the point of view, predicament, or plight of the individual. All men on this basis are intrinsically worthful as brothers because of the fact of origin rather than of the subsequent condition of life.

Each man then stands in immediate candidacy for the activated feeling of brotherliness toward every other man. The mood of brotherliness, therefore, is not merely created by conformity to ethics, morality, or value judgments, but is grounded in a gross awareness of the life process itself. When this awareness is heightened to the point that it becomes the formal basis of operation for the individual, that which men are in seed, they become in deed.

The Will to Understand

The will to understand other people is a most important part of the personal equipment of those who would share in the unfolding ideal of human fellowship. It is not enough merely to be sincere, to be conscientious. This is not to underestimate the profound necessity for sincerity in human relations, but it is to point out the fact that sincerity is no substitute for intelligent understanding.

The will to understand requires an authentic sense of fact with reference to as many areas of human life as possible. This means that we must use the raw materials of accurate knowledge of others to give strength and direction to the will to understand. A healthy skepticism with reference to rumors, gossip, what we read and observe about others, must be ever present, causing all these things to be evaluated by our own highly developed sense of fact.

It is easy to say that we understand other persons whose culture and background are different from ours, merely because we are kind to them or willing to make personal sacrifices on their behalf. A certain Spaniard, commenting on the difference between a cat and a dog, says that a dog is direct, obvious in his expression of friendliness, while a cat, when he rubs against you, is not caressing you, but merely caressing himself against you. How apropos!

Unless there is a constant heightening of the sense of fact to give guidance to our will to understand, we are apt to substitute sentimentality for understanding, softness for tenderness, and weakness for strength in human relations.

"Friends Whom I Knew Not"

Thou hast made known to me friends whom I knew not
Thou hast brought the distant near and made a brother of the stranger.

The strength of the personal life is often found in the depth and intensity of its isolation. The fight for selfhood is unending. There is the ever-present need to stand alone, unsupported and unchallenged. To be sure of one's self, to be counted for one's self *as* one's self, is to experience aliveness in its most exciting dimension. If there is a job of work to be done that is impossible, if there is a need to be met that is limitless, if there is a word to be said that can never be said, the spirit of the whole man is mustered and in the exhaustive effort he finds *himself* in the solitariness of strength renewed and courage regained.

Below the surface of all the activity and functioning in which life engages us, there is a level of disengagement when the individual is a private actor on a lonely stage. It is here that things are seen without their outer garbs—the seedlings of desires take quiet root, the bitter waters and the sweet springs find their beginnings, the tiny stirrings that become the raging tempests are seen to shimmer in the semi-darkness—this is "the region," "the place," "the clime," where man is the lonely, solitary guest in the vast empty house of the world.

But this is not all of a person's life, this is not the full and solid picture. The strands of life cannot be so divided that each can be traced to a separate source. There is no mine, there is no thine. When there is that which I would claim as my very own, a second look, a subtle strangeness, something, announces that there can never be anything that is my very own. Always moving in upon a person's life is the friend whose existence he did not know, whose coming and going is not his to determine.

The journeyings take many forms—sometimes it is in the vista that opens before his mind because of lines written long before in an age he did not know; sometimes it is in a simple encounter along the way when before his eyes the unknown stranger becomes the sharer of tidings that could be borne only by a friend. Sometimes a deep racial memory throws into focus an ancient wisdom that steadies the hand and stabilizes the heart. Always moving in upon a person's life is the friend whose existence he did not know, whose coming and going is not his to determine. At last, a person's life is his very own *and* a person's life is never his, alone.

"We Are All One"

Long ago, Plotinus wrote, "If we are in unity with the Spirit, we are in unity with each other, and so we are all one." The words of this ancient Greek mystic are suggestive, for they call attention to the underlying unity of all life. The recognition of the Spirit of God as the unifying principle of all life becomes at once the most crucial experience of man. It says that whoever is aware of the Spirit of God in himself enters the doors that lead into the life of his fellows.

The same idea is stated in ethical terms in the New Testament when the suggestion is made that, if a man says he loves God, whom he hath not seen, and does not love his brother who is with him, he is a liar and the truth does not dwell in him. The way is difficult, because it is very comforting to withdraw from the responsibility of unity with one's fellows and to enter alone into the solitary contemplation of God.

One can have a perfect orgy of solitary communion without the risks of being misunderstood, of having one's words twisted, of having to be on the defensive about one's true or alleged attitude. In the quiet fellowship with one's God, one may seem to be relieved of any necessity to make headway against heavy odds. This is why one encounters persons of deep piousness and religiosity who are intolerant and actively hostile toward their fellows. Some of the most terrifying hate organizations in the country are made up in large part of persons who are very devout in the worship of their God.

The test to which Plotinus puts us, however, is very searching. To be in unity with the Spirit is to be in unity with one's fellows. Not to be in unity with one's fellows is thereby not to be in unity with the Spirit. The pragmatic test of one's unity with the Spirit is found in the unity with one's fellows. We see what this means when we are involved in the experience of a broken relationship.

When I have lost harmony with another, my whole life is thrown out of tune. God tends to be remote and far away when a desert and sea appear between me and another. I draw close to God as I draw close to my fellows. The great incentive remains ever alert; I cannot be at peace without God, and I cannot be truly aware of God if I am not at peace with my fellows. For the sake of my unity with God, I keep working on my relations with my fellows. This is ever the insistence of all ethical religions.

She Practices Brotherhood

The telephone rang at seven-fifteen in the morning. And on the other end was a lady whose voice seemed full of years, soft but strong. What she had to say was profoundly stirring: "I am sorry to disturb you so early in the morning, but I wanted to call you before you left the hotel for the day.

"About ten years ago (I am now sixty-nine) I decided to examine my life to see what, if anything, I could do to put into practice my own convictions about brotherhood. Why I decided this, and not suddenly, I need not say. But I did. The first thing I discovered was that I knew almost nothing about other races in my own city, particularly about Negroes. I went to the library and was given a small list of books and magazines. I began to work. The things I learned!

When it seemed to me that I had my hands on enough facts (and I discovered you don't need too many facts, because they get in your way), I plotted a course of action.

"Then I was stumped. What could I do? I had no particular abilities, very little energy, and an extremely modest income. But I did like to talk with people as I met them on the buses and in the stores. I decided that I would spread the facts I had and my own concern among all the people whose lives were touched by mine in direct conversation. It took me some time to develop a simple approach that would not be an intrusion or a discourtesy. For several years, I have been doing this on the bus riding into town each week, in a department store where I have made my purchases for two decades, and in various other places.

"Occasionally, I run into a person in the street who stops to introduce himself and to remind me of a previous meeting. One such person said, 'I guess you have forgotten, but about four years ago I sat by you on a bus, and I don't know how the question came up but we talked about the Negroes; and you started me thinking along lines that had never occurred to me. You even gave me the name of a book which I noted and purchased. Since then, I have been instrumental in changing the whole personnel practice of our business on this question. Thanks to you!' "

Continuing, she said: "I know that this is not very much and I guess many people are doing much more. But I thought I would tell you this so that, in your moments of discouragement, you may remember what one simple old lady was doing to help in little ways to right big wrongs. Good-by and God bless you." She did not give me her name, nor her address; she merely shared her testimony and gave her witness.

"No Man Is an Island"

"No man is an island," no man lives alone. The words from a poem by John Donne have been set to music and have become the theme of a variety of radio programs which are concerned with aspects of social responsibility.

It is of crucial importance for each person to consider how he relates himself to the society of which, of necessity, he is a part. For many people and, at times, for most of us, it is a part of our dreaming to be let alone, to be free of all involvements in the responsibilities of life and for others. This is but natural; often the mood passes. Sometimes we say that our personal load is so heavy that it is all we can do to look after ourselves, with all that that entails. Even as we express such ideas, we are reminded by a wide variety of events that we are never ourselves alone. We are not an island, we do not live alone.

There is no alternative to the insistence that we cannot escape from personal responsibility for the social order in which we live. We are a part of the society in which we function. There can be no health for us if we lose our sense of personal responsibility for the social order. This means that there must be participation in the social process, and that quite specifically. Such participation means the wise and critical use of the ballot; the registering of our intent to share responsibility in government.

The moral inference is that there must not be a condemnation of the political process of society if we have been unwilling to stand up and be counted on behalf of the kind of government in which we believe and for which we are willing to work and sacrifice. Where social change seems to be urgent, we must share in that process as responsible, law-abiding citizens.

The ethical values by which we live must be implemented on the level of social change. This calls ever for a careful evaluation of the means to which we give our support. The means which we are willing to use must not be in real conflict with the ends which our values inspire. Practically, this means that if we believe in democracy, for instance, we must not be a party to means that make use of bigotry, prejudice, and hate. We must search and find the facts that are needed for judgment and cast our lot on the side of the issues which we are willing to embrace as our private and personal ends. In working on behalf of such ends, which are morally right as we see the right, we shall not cooperate with or be a party to means that seem to us evil—means that we would not use in our personal private life.

We are our brother's keeper; for we will not demand of any man that he do on behalf of society as a whole what as persons we would be loath to do ourselves if we were in his place.

"For We Know in Part"

"For we know in part, and we prophesy in part . . ."
The sense of self is fully known
When a man can say, "I did it."
Such triumph who can claim?
In every deed are many streams
Whose sources lie beyond all dreams,
Or sleep within the womb of ancient myths.

The words in his tongue, wanderers all,
Finding in man a short-spanned place—
They're never his alone.
O'er what a way they've come!
Through countless years in every land,
Through crucibles of every mood
Words now familiar in their place
Have made their own the marks of many minds.
How dare a man say, "I—I speak"?

Free-flowing thoughts from living minds
Are big with residues of other times
Forced from their place by inner law,
Compelled to rest in little spells;
A man may never say, "This thought is mine."
An equity in thoughts is his;
The rest belongs to every man.

Fierce, private, intimate, unique
Feelings spring from deep within;
A boundless inner world as old as life—
They come, without command.
The feeling tone, the pointed shape
Carries the image of the man.
To this he gives his own life's plan,
No more than this is his to claim.

All knowledge in whatever form

Maintains its place, secure.
It knows no lord, no single mind.
Its harvest ripens as it will.
Its secret is its own to give,
In part, to share with other minds.
To say "I know" is always false,
However sure the words may seem.
Before the echo fades, the lights go out,
The man is held by fear, by doubt.
To seek, to find, to seek again,
This is man's journey, this his way.

The Strange Glory

Always there seems to be a restlessness at the very center of personality. This is no matter of mere temperament. True, there are those who give the sudden disapproval of everything, looking with quick and muted anger at anything that seeks the approval of their nod. Here is a disposition or attitude that seems to be rooted in the subsoil of the character, the seeds of which were sown by an errant wind when life was early and the soil was right. Or perhaps it is the bruised reaction to a moment of violence or the pain of promises broken when all of one's hopes rode on the grand anticipation of fulfillment. Or it may be malfunctioning of some part of the organism that uses its share of bodily energy while withholding its contribution to the total health and weal. But this is not the restlessness and unease of the center, of the core.

What is here in mind is the residue that is left when the best is given, when the duty is fulfilled, when the task is completed. This is the strange torture and glory of the human spirit. A man accepts a responsibility. He puts at its disposal his abilities, his skills, all of the rich resources of his mind and his spirit. In meeting the responsibility he has a sense of sharing in the *meaning* of meaning. When the work is done what he sees is good and he knows that he has worked worthily and effectively. And yet he cannot come to a place of rest about it. There is no particular thing that he can point to that yields the character of the flaw. What has been done is good and there is no negative judgment about it, only the residue in his spirit that cannot be contained by the goodness and the integrity of the deed.

Or here is a man who gives himself to, and is accepted by, some Cause, which Cause is more important to him than his own life, than whether he lives or dies. Yet when he has emptied himself, holding back nothing from the searching and imperious demand of his Purpose, something remains, some sense of limitation, perhaps, or inadequacy perhaps . . . something . . . Incidents or illustrations multiply themselves; always with the same underlying results.

Man is more than his body and his mind. Man is more than the particular deed or the most astounding total of all his deeds. Man is more than the fulfillment of his dreams or the realization of his hopes. Man is earthbound but something deep within him is always transcending the earth, moving meaningfully among the stars. He is finite and infinite, he is bounded and boundless, he is human and divine. He is a space binder and a time binder.

> Heir of the Kingdom 'neath the skies
> Often he falls, yet falls to rise;
> Stumbling, bleeding, beaten back
> Holding still to the upward track;
> Playing his part in creation's plan
> God-like in image, this is man.

Life Becomes Personal

The quality of reconciliation is that of wholeness; it seeks to effect and further harmonious relations in a totally comprehensive climate.

The concern for reconciliation finds expression in the simple human desire to understand others and to be understood by others. These are the building blocks of the society of man, the precious ingredients without which man's life is a nightmare and the future of his life on the planet doomed.

Every man wants to be cared for, to be sustained by the assurance that he shares in the watchful and thoughtful attention of others—not merely or necessarily others in general but others in particular. He wants to know that—however vast and impersonal all life about him may seem, however hard may be the stretch of road on which he is journeying—he is not alone, but the object of another's concern and caring; wants to know this in an awareness sufficient to hold him against ultimate fear and panic. It is precisely at this point of awareness that life becomes personal and the individual a person. Through it he gets some intimation of what, after all, he finally amounts to, and the way is cleared for him to experience his own spirit.

Our Little Lives

Our little lives, our big problems—these we place upon Thy altar!
Each of us, an assortment of vast mixtures!
The quietness in Thy Temple of Silence again and again rebuffs us:
For some there is no discipline to hold us steady in the waiting
And the minds reject the noiseless invasion of Thy spirit.
For some there is no will to offer what is central in the thoughts—
The confusion is so manifest, there is no starting place to take hold.
For some the evils of the world tear down all concentrations
And scatter the focus of the high resolves.
    War and the threat of war has covered us with heavy shadows,
    Making the days big with forebodings—
    The nights crowded with frenzied dreams and restless churnings.
    We do not know how to do what we know to do.
    We do not know how to be what we know to be.
Our little lives, our big problems—these we place upon Thy altar!
Brood over our spirits, our Father,
Blow upon whatever dream Thou hast for us
That there may glow once again upon our hearths,
The fire of Thy contagion.
Pour out upon us whatever our spirits need of shock, of lift, of release
That we may find strength for these days—
Courage and hope for tomorrow.
In confidence we rest in Thy sustaining grace
Which makes possible triumph in defeat, gain in loss, and love in hate.
We rejoice this day to say:
Our little lives, our big problems—these we place upon Thy altar!

When the Strain Is Heaviest

At times when the strain is heaviest upon us,
And our tired nerves cry out in many-tongued pain
Because the flow of love is choked far below the deep recesses of the
    heart,
We seek with cravings firm and hard
The strength to break the dam
That we may live again in love's warm stream.
We want more love; and more and more,
Until at last we are restored and made anew!
Or, so it seems.

When we are closer drawn to God's great Light
And in its radiance stand revealed,
The meaning of our need informs our minds.
"More love," we cried; as if love could be weighed, measured,
    bundled, tied.
As if with perfect wisdom we could say—to one, a little love; to
    another, an added portion;
And on and on until all debts are paid, with no one left behind.

But now we see the tragic blunder of our cry.
Not for more love our hungry cravings seek!
But more power to love.
To put behind the tender feeling, the understanding heart,
The boundless reaches of the Father's care
Makes love eternal, always kindled, always new.
This becomes the eager meaning of the aching heart,
The bitter cry—the anguish call!

Lord, Lord, Open Unto Me

Open unto me—light for
        my darkness
Open unto me—courage for
        my fear

Open unto me—hope for
　　my despair
Open unto me—peace for
　　my turmoil
Open unto me—joy for
　　my sorrow
Open unto me—strength for
　　my weakness
Open unto me—wisdom for
　　my confusion
Open unto me—forgiveness for
　　my sins
Open unto me—tenderness for
　　my toughness
Open unto me—love for
　　my hates
Open unto me—Thy Self for
　　my self

Lord, Lord, Open Unto Me

Making a Good Life

There is much conversation about making a good life. Deep within the human spirit is a concern that insists upon perfection. The distinction must be made between perfection in a particular activity, in a particular skill, and the central concern of the human spirit for perfection as a total experience. The former can be measured in terms of standards and concrete goals. I know a man who is most meticulous about many things that have their place but are inconsequential. He is so insistent about the temperature of his coffee that he neglects simple courtesy to the person who serves it.

Sometimes the attitude is more comprehensive. It has to do with staking out an area and covering it in a certain way with a satisfactory structure. It has to do with plans and their fulfillment—ends and the means by which the ends are secured. This kind of perfection often makes for arrogance of spirit and unbearable snobbery. It says to all and sundry: There is but one way to do a thing and this is that way. It does not always follow that arrogance is the result; there may be a simple pride in the beauty and the wholeness of the flawless. To behold a lovely thing in all its parts, be it a deed, a well-rounded idea, a clear, beautiful, and perfect phrase, or a way of performing, is to experience a moment of glory and sheer delight.

But the central concern for perfection lies outside of all manifestations and all deeds. It is more than, and other than, all expressions of every kind, and yet it informs the ultimate character of all expressions of every kind. It is the image which the sculptor sees in the block of marble; the dream in the soul of the prophet and the seer; the profound sense of life in the spirit of the dying; the picture of the beloved in the eyes of the lover; the hope that continues when all rational grounds for confidence have been destroyed. It is what remains when all doors have finally closed and all the lights have gone out, one by one.

Here at last we are face to face with what man is in his literal substance: the essence of his nobility and dignity. In religion it is called the image of the Creator and is the authentic "for instance" of the givenness of God. To be aware of this is the source of all man's confidential endurance through the vicissitudes of his living. This is to sit in judgment on every deed, however good and perfect it may be within itself—to move with reverence through all of life, always seeking and finding, always building and rebuilding, always repenting, always rejoicing. This is to walk with God.

New Wood

It was a simple story told to his graduating class by a quiet, soft-spoken college president who, for many years, had poured his life into the deepest needs of generations of young college women. He had inherited from his father the farm upon which the days of his childhood were spent. On the farm was an apple tree, older than a half century. He had noticed that the clue to the perennial fruit of the tree was the fact that each year's fruit grew only on that year's wood. This law of its life faced the tree with a very searching option: it must grow new wood every year if it expected to bear fruit that year. If it did not bear fruit, it could not fulfill its destiny. It could continue to live—there would be life in the old wood and that life would bring forth leaves—but that is all. If there would be fruit on the tree, there must be new wood. This year's apples could not grow on last year's wood.

How often in our own experiences do we make demands upon old wood that can be made only upon new wood. This year's fruit can grow only on this year's wood. If for any reason fruit does not grow on this year's wood, then its day was yesterday, its year was yesteryear. There is a function of last year's wood; that function is to produce this year's wood. But the fruit can grow only on this year's wood.

Age has its uses. There is a wisdom of experience and a vast strength that belong to that which has borne its fruit in its time. Often we forget this. We expect the time of fruitbearing to wait for our convenience, our mood, our permissions. We cling to the old way, the old pattern, because they were good in their time. Again and again we utter the complaint of the old wood—last year or ten years ago we did it this way. The favorite phrase is, "I remember when . . ." Even in very intimate and personal ways we are often bound by the lament of the old wood: "This is the way my father did it," or "This is how I grew up." We forget that each year's fruit must grow on that year's wood. Our responsibility is not to bear fruit, it would seem. Our responsibility is to grow new wood. The laws of life will bring the fruit. Such is also the common failure of organizations. The old-timers, who had one time been in power and who bore rich fruit in their time, find it difficult often to grow new wood for this year's fruit. There is a necessitous function for old wood, without which there can be no new growth. Wisdom is in knowing what that function is. The function of the old is to grow the new wood upon which this year's fruit can move from blossom to ripeness. To refuse to grow new wood is to put one's self against life! It is to retreat from life; it is to die.

This year's fruit grows only on this year's wood.

"Knowledge . . . Shall Vanish Away"

Whether there be knowledge, it shall vanish away. . . .
A ceaseless search like the ebb and flow of oceans
Marks all man's days:
For him no rest, no rest;

The fever in the blood
Is answer to the temper of the mind.

When Time was young, just learning how to walk,
It placed its stamp on the single cell
Which gave a slant to all that lives
Today or yesterday, no matter when.
A ceaseless search like the ebb and flow of oceans
Marks all man's day.

Is there some point, some place of rest
To bring an end to all man's quest?
Something that does not fail?
Something that lasts beyond all things that pass
When shadows thicken and the lights grow dim?
Some worldly hope that gives retreat
From all the winds that beat upon the world?
Some sure attachment to another's life
That stands secure against all change of mind or heart?
Some private dream where only dwells
The purest secrets of desire?
All these must fade,
All these must pass away.

There is a sense of wholeness at the core of man
That must abound in all he does;
That marks with reverence his ev'ry step;
That has its sway when all else fails;
That wearies out all evil things;
That warms the depth of frozen fears
Making friend of foe,
Making love of hate,
And lasts beyond the living and the dead,
Beyond the goals of peace, the ends of war!
This man seeks through all his years:
To be complete and of one piece, within, without.

The Integrity of the Person

There is something strangely comforting and reassuring about the private pretensions under which we live. It is a matter of no little significance to know that for each of us there is a world apart in which the intimacy of thoughts and feelings may be safe from attack and violation. Much of what we mean by communication is limited to the deliberate choosing of thoughts, ideas, sentiments, feelings, which we direct toward others—yielding only the meaning that we intend, which may not be the meaning that is either true or honest. In time we develop a dependence upon the impact which we make on others as the major source from which we draw an understanding of ourselves.

I am impressed by the stories which have come to us concerning the life of the American Indian at a time far removed from the present. To him, so the accounts reveal, the Great Spirit brooded over all of life in general and particular. Before he went hunting, he invoked the Great Spirit. When crops were planted, when there was death and birth, he invoked the Great Spirit. In fine, all the common and special experiences of life were seen as being under the scrutiny and sponsorship of the Great Spirit. This meant that there was ever available the opportunity and the necessity for being genuine—the wall between the inner and the outer was very thin and transparent. *The integrity of the act* sprang out of *the integrity of the person.* There was no need to pretend. One dare not pretend to the Great Spirit.

A crushing part of the sophistication of modern life is the phenomenal rise in the feeling for a protective covering that will make the integrity of the act an awkward procedure. Why is it that we are embarrassed by simple honesty and directness in our communication with one another? And yet the hunger deepens and becomes more and more insistent for ridding ourselves of the tremendous burden of pretensions. We long for relationships in which it is no longer needful for us to pretend anything. The clue to the answer is in the awakening within us of the sense of living our lives consciously in God's presence. The habit of exposing the life, the motives, the dreams, the desires, the sins, all to God makes for *the integrity of the person.* Out of this flows *the integrity of the act.*

> Search me, O God, and know my heart,
> Try me, and know my thoughts.

Life's Working Paper

For every man there is a necessity to establish as securely as possible the lines along which he proposes to live his life. In developing his life's working paper, he must take into account many factors, in his reaction to which he may seem to throw them out of line with their true significance. As a man, he did not happen. He was born, he has a name, he has forebears, he is the product of a particular culture, he has a mother tongue, he belongs to a nation, he is born into some kind of faith. In addition to all of these, he exists, in some curious way, as a person independent of all other facts. There is an intensely private world, all his own; it is intimate, exclusive, sealed.

The life working paper of the individual is made up of a creative synthesis of what the man is in all his parts and how he reacts to the living processes. It is wide of the mark to say that a man's working paper is ever wrong; it may not be fruitful, it may be negative, but it is never wrong. For such a judgment would imply that the synthesis is guaranteed to be of a certain kind, of a specific character, resulting in a foreordained end. It can never be determined just what a man will fashion.

Two men may be born of the same parents, grow up in the same environment, be steeped in the same culture, and inspired by the same faith. Close or even cursory observation may reveal that each has fashioned a life working paper so unique that different roads are taken, and each day the two men grow farther and farther apart. Or it may be that they move along precisely parallel lines that never meet.

Always, then, there is the miracle of the working paper. Whenever there appears in human history a personality whose story is available and whose reach extends far in all directions, the question of his working paper is as crucial as is the significance of his life. We want to know what were the lines along which he decided to live his life. How did he relate himself to the central issues of his time? What were the questions which he had to answer? Was he under some necessity to give a universal character to his most private experience?

"Make Me Big"

An unknown poet has written:

> Each night my bonny, sturdy lad
> Persists in adding to his, Now I lay me
> Down to sleep, the earnest, wistful plea:
> "God make me big."
> And I, his mother, with a greater need,
> Do echo in an humbled, contrite heart,
> "God make me big."

The simple desire of the average child is to become a big boy or girl. Time seems to stand still or to move backward. Particularly is that true in families where there are several children or even two children of different ages. Sometimes the older child has more privileges, more freedom of movement, is treated in an adult manner by parents. All of this inspires in the younger the burning desire to move into a higher age bracket in order that the joys of riper years may be his. This is a most natural development and as such does not call for any special comment.

But what the poet has in mind is something much more deeply interfused in the quest of the human spirit for a quality of life that is equal to the vicissitudes of experience. Many instances come to mind. Some person takes advantage of you in a situation and you are powerless to protect yourself or your interest. Days pass. Then, one day, the tables are turned and your most urgent impulse is to even the score. Much rationalization takes place. "I knew my turn would come," you say to yourself; "now I'll show him how it feels. Turnabout is fair play, anyway. Besides, it is a bad idea for people to feel that they can do what he did to me and get away with it."— "God make me big," you whisper, as you turn aside from the temptation for revenge.

Or it may be that you have impressed people with your ability or your genuineness of interest in an enterprise. You are faced with the opportunity to do a really significant job involving heavy responsibility. You cower in the presence of it. "I can't do that. I am not equal to it." Or, "I really am not interested in it to that extent." But there it is, and you have no available alternative but to tackle it.

"God make me big," you cry out with all the power of your spirit. And then a strange thing happens. Strength comes from somewhere. The job does not seem so hard as it did before you tackled it. Deep within the task, something is released that eases the load; and the quality of your performance pervades your spirit with the assurance that God has answered. SO!

A Sense of Fancy

It is exceedingly difficult to live one's life creatively and effectively without developing what may be called a sense of fancy. An important distinction must be made between a sense of fancy and a sense of fact. A sense of fancy seems to be the particular gift of little children. They people the world with living fairies and elves; the little girl carries on a real conversation with her doll; Santa Claus does come down the chimney, and he has reindeer and a sleigh, and he does live at the North Pole, spending all the time between Christmases making toys for little girls and boys.

Of course, if this sort of thing persists into manhood and womanhood, the individual may be regarded as being somewhat off-balance. But what is basically present in a sense of fancy must continue to influence the attitude and outlook of the individual toward the world and toward people. This unique element has to do with imagination, with the ability to envision things in terms of their highest meaning and fulfillment, even as one grapples with them in the present as they are. It is not to disregard the sordid, the mean, the thing of low estate in one's life, or one's experiences with others, but it is to deal with these aspects of life in the light of their highest possibility.

The sense of fancy then broods over the meanness of man until there begins to appear in one's relationship with him, growing edges that are full of promise—that are not mean. I repeat, it is not to ignore the fact that the man is mean or devilish or prejudiced, but it is to recognize that this in itself is not a complete picture of the man. There is something more there. A developed sense of fancy illumines the dark reaches of the other person until there is brought to light that which makes for wholeness and beauty in him. This is what God is doing in human life all the time.

The Place Where You Live

It is a simple story, simply told. One day, a man walked into an antique shop and asked permission to look around. It was a rather exclusive shop frequented only by those who could afford to purchase articles made rare by their scarcity and age. The visitor seemed strangely out of place because he was poorly dressed, though clean; indeed it was clear from his appearance that he was a laborer whose face had been etched by sun and rain and whose hands were rough and worn. After more than a half hour, he left.

In about ten days he returned. This time he found a very beautiful piece of old glass and asked if he could make a deposit on it. Each week he made a payment, until at last the article was his. With much curiosity, the owner of the shop engaged him in conversation to determine, if he could, the use to which such a man would put his new purchase.

"I bought it for my little room. It isn't much, but I bring to it, from time to time, through the years, only the very best and most beautiful things. You see, that is where I *live*."

To bring to the place where you live only the best and most beautiful—what a plan for one's life! This is well within the reach of everyone. Think of using one's memory in that way. As one lives from day to day, there are all sorts of experiences, good, bad, beautiful, ugly, that become a part of one's past. To develop the ability to screen one's memory so that only the excellent is retained for one's own room! All kinds of ideas pass through one's mind, about oneself, about the world, about people. Which do you keep for your own room? Think it over now; which ideas do you keep for the place where you live?

It is well within the mark to say that the oft-quoted words of Jesus, about laying up for yourself treasures in heaven, deal with this same basic idea. The place where you live is where your treasures are. Where your treasures are is where your heart is. Where your heart is, is where your God is.

Keep Alive the Dream in the Heart

As long as a man has a dream in his heart, he cannot lose the significance of living.

It is a part of the pretensions of modern life to traffic in what is generally called "realism." There is much insistence upon being practical, down to earth. Such things as dreams are wont to be regarded as romantic or as a badge of immaturity, or as escape hatches for the human spirit. When such a mood or attitude is carefully scrutinized, it is found to be made up largely of pretensions, in short, of bluff. Men cannot continue long to live if the dream in the heart has perished. It is then that they stop hoping, stop looking, and the last embers of their anticipations fade away.

The dream in the heart is the outlet. It is one with the living water welling up from the very springs of Being, nourishing and sustaining all of life. Where there is no dream, the life becomes a swamp, a dreary dead place, and deep within, a man's heart begins to rot. The dream need not be some great and overwhelming plan; it need not be a dramatic picture of what might or must be someday; it need not be a concrete outpouring of a world-shaking possibility of sure fulfillment. Such may be important for some; such may be crucial for a particular moment of human history. But it is not in these grand ways that the dream nourishes life.

The dream is the quiet persistence in the heart that enables a man to ride out the storms of his churning experiences. It is the exciting whisper moving through the aisles of his spirit answering the monotony of limitless days of dull routine. It is the ever-recurring melody in the midst of the broken harmony and harsh discords of human conflict. It is the touch of significance which highlights the ordinary experience, the common event. The dream is no outward thing. It does not take its rise from the environment in which one moves or functions. It lives in the inward parts, it is deep within, where the issues of life and death are ultimately determined.

Keep alive the dream; for as long as a man has a dream in his heart, he cannot lose the significance of living.

To Which Loyalty Are You True?

It is never quite possible to resolve in a manner that is completely satisfying the conflict between loyalties. There is the conflict between loyalty to the ideal of mercy on the one hand and loyalty to the ideal of literal truthtelling on the other.

In Henry van Dyke's story, *The Other Wise Man,* there is an account of one experience which the Other Wise Man had with Herod's soldiers. He came to a court within which was a cottage. When he entered the cottage he found a young woman and her male child hiding in a corner. Herod had dispatched his soldiers to kill all male children under a certain age. When the leader of a small group of soldiers appeared at the door of the cottage, he asked the Other Wise Man, "Is there a male child in this house?" Whereupon the reply came back directly: "No." And the child's life was spared.

If you had been at the door, to which loyalty would you have been true? Perhaps if it were your own child there would be no question. I wonder.

Or consider the conflict between loyalty to an ultimate goal and loyalty to an immediate goal, both of which are good but one seems to be better than the other, though more remote. The platitude, A bird in the hand is worth two in the bush, is one answer. How often do we seize upon the immediate good because it is within reach and thereby sacrifice the better thing because the time interval is so great that we fear we shall die before we realize it! To escape the risk of losing all, we accept what is available.

The issue becomes clearer when we apply it to a concrete situation. A man runs for a political office. Standing outside of the responsibility of the office, it is clear to him which is the right, the ideal thing to do. When he is elected, he becomes a man with the responsibility of office and, all his days, he wrestles with the loyalty to his ideals and loyalty to the responsibilities of office.

Power always involves a man in a network of compromises. This is true because a man has to be selfless in relation to his ideals or be destroyed by them. Power always includes more than the private relation between a man and his personal ideals. To give up the struggle is to lose one's soul. And what would a man give in exchange for his soul? Fame? Prestige? Glory? Power?

The Experience of Growing Up

Always the experience of growing up teaches the same lesson:
The hard way of self-reliance—the uneasy tensions of self-
  confidence.
What there is to be done in accordance with the persistent
  desire,
Each must do for himself.
Often by trial and error, by fumblings and blunderings,
Here a little, there a little more,
Step by uncertain step we move in the direction of self-
  awareness:
Gathering unto ourselves a personal flavor, a tang of unique-
  ness.
In this strength of intimate disclosure, each person faces his
  world,
Does battle with nameless forces,
Conquers and is defeated, wins or loses, waxes strong or
  weak.
Always experience says, "Rely on your own strength, hold
  fast to your own resources, desert not your own mind."
In the same sure moment, the same voice whispers, "Upon
  your own strength, upon your own resource, upon your
  own mind,
At long last you cannot rely.
Your own strength is weakness
Your own mind is shallow
Your own spirit is feeble."
The paradox:
All experience strips us of much except our sheer strength of
  mind, of spirit.
All experience reveals that upon these we must not finally
  depend.
Brooding over us and about us, even in the shadows of the
  paradox, there is something more—
There is a strength beyond our strength, giving strength to
  our strength.

Whether we bow our knee before an altar or
Spend our days in the delusions of our significance,
The unalterable picture remains the same;
Sometimes in the stillness of the quiet, if we listen,
We can hear the whisper in the heart
Giving strength to weakness, courage to fear, hope to despair.

The Glad Surprise

There is ever something compelling and exhilarating about the glad surprise. The emphasis is upon *glad*. There are surprises that are shocking, startling, frightening, and bewildering. But the glad surprise is something different from all of these. It carries with it the element of elation, of life, of something over and beyond the surprise itself.

The experience itself comes at many levels: the simple joy that comes when one discovers that the balance in the bank is larger than the personal record indicated—and there is no error in accounting; the realization that one does not have his door key—the hour is late and everyone is asleep—but someone very thoughtfully left the latch off, "just in case"; the dreaded meeting in a conference to work out some problems of misunderstanding, and things are adjusted without the emotional lacerations anticipated; the report from the doctor's examination that all is well, when one was sure that the physical picture was very serious indeed. All of these surprises are glad!

The concept of the glad surprise has a deeper meaning. It has to do with the very ground and foundation of hope about the nature of life itself. The manifestation of this quality in the world about us can best be witnessed in the coming of spring. It is ever a new thing, a glad surprise, the stirring of life at the end of winter. One day there seems to be no sign of life and then almost overnight, swelling buds, delicate blooms, blades of grass, bugs, insects—an entire world of newness everywhere. It is the glad surprise at the end of winter.

Often the same experience comes at the end of a long tunnel of tragedy and tribulation. It is as if a man stumbling in the darkness, having lost his way, finds that the spot at which he falls is the foot of a stairway that leads from darkness into light. Such is the glad surprise.

This is what Easter means in the experience of the race. This is the resurrection! It is the announcement that life cannot ultimately be conquered by death, that there is no road that is at last swallowed up in an ultimate darkness, that there is strength added when the labors increase, that multiplied peace matches multiplied trials, that life is bottomed by the glad surprise. Take courage, therefore:

> When we have exhausted our store of endurance,
> When our strength has failed ere the day is half done,
> When we reach the end of our hoarded resources,
> Our Father's full giving is only begun.

Man Cannot Be Indifferent to Men

The key to community must be fashioned of a common understanding of life, a common faith, a common commitment.

Every person is at long last concerned with community. A persistent strain in the human spirit rejects the experience of isolation as being alien to its genius. It is true that there are moments when the feeling for aloneness, for solitariness, must be honored and respected. Every person has said many times over, "I must get away from it all. I want to be alone." This really means the urgency to catch up with one's self, to clear the bearings, that one's true place in community may be more accurately seen and realized.

But community is the native climate of the human spirit. It is for this reason that we seem most our true selves when we are deeply involved in relations with other selves. Man cannot be indifferent to men. The human race cannot be ignored by the individual man. However skilled a man may be in a particular field of endeavor, however effective he may be in doing a job, there can be no peace of mind until such a man establishes an authentic sense of community with his fellows. He begins always at the primary level. He wants to be related specifically and privately to others. He must share in a common understanding of life with others or another like himself. He must be a part of a common faith with others or another like himself. This is the level at which community begins. It builds outward to include more and more of a man's fellows—but it begins at the primary level.

Wherever community at this level is ruptured, some precious part of the self perishes. It is for this reason that the experience of forgiveness, of restoration, plays so crucial a part in the life of every man. It is of the primary relation with individuals that the bridge connecting one to a group or groups is constructed. Always a man is driven to do something about his personal relationships. He must have free and easy access to persons who are immediately significant to him if he is to share deeply in community. This is the very stuff upon which the soul of man feeds; for it is the door through which he enters into the Holy of Holies where God dwells. For behold the dwelling place of God is in the hearts of men! This is the tug of God that pulls each of us to Him. The most direct response is through the *human* heart: my own heart and the hearts of my fellows.

The Quickening Possibility

> We plod,
> Tongue-tied and deaf, along life's common road
> But suddenly, we know not how, a sound
> Of living streams, an odour, a flower crowned
> With dew, a lark upspringing from the sod,
> And we awake.

It is thus that Edward Dowden describes the quickening possibilities of life. The daily round is often so full of sameness that the monotony of routine seeps into our very spirits. Each succeeding day is like the day that preceded it, until at last they fuse into one continuous interval of dullness.

Or it may be that the level of our expectancy in life is so low that we become immune to possibilities beyond that which is contained in the passing moment. It is entirely possible so to live that there is no anticipation of something beyond our immediate demands. When this is our tempo, our very citadel has to be stormed by some tremendous event, some spectacular invasion of our senses, or some sudden jeopardy to our sense of casual well-being before we can spill over into experiences that take us "beyond our immediate demand." When this happens, we may call it a miracle of coincidence—the experience extraordinary.

It is important to remember, however, that life all about us is full of the moments which, without warning, may become the rare moment in which the individual may become awakened to much, much more than he had ever dreamed as being possible for him. It need not be some startling disclosure coming on the wings of a great insight— it may be a shaft of light picking up colors in a piece of rock; it may be the solitary voice of a bird alone on the branch of a tree, singing his morning song; it may be a face encountered in a crowded street- car; it may be a word spoken by a friend illuminating it with a rush of new meaning and fresh insight; it may be the taste of food that moves through all the reaches of the senses, making magic out of bread and the eating thereof.

Or it may be an impulse to do a kindness which unlocks a hidden door opening into a veritable treasure house of riches never before even guessed. The only thing we know is that as we live from day to day, we are ever in candidacy for the moment which may be for us *the* moment that awakens us to much, much more than what has gone before. How wonderful it is to keep the level of expectancy high, to the end that our lives may not be smothered by the routine of our days!

The Climate of Acceptance

It is easy in the world to live after the world's opinion; it is easy in solitude to live after our own; but the great man is he who in the midst of the crowd keeps with perfect sweetness the independence of solitude. . . .

A great measure of comfort and reassurance is derived from feeling one's self surrounded by a familiar climate of acceptance. To be approved of is far more important than to approve. To do nothing that raises a question or threatens rejection is safe and deadly. Always to defer to the opinion of "the others"; always to give in to what "they" want or what "they" think; always to be guided by the mother's hand—this is to conform, this is to live the automatic life.

A great measure of comfort and reassurance is derived from feeling one's self to be free of others and their opinions. How good it is to be faced with no judgmental attitudes other than one's own. If it could be achieved, there are times when every one of us would flee into solitude where all reckonings are one's own, where there is no voice to be heard save one's own, where no reactions are in evidence save one's own. This would be to live with the freedom that is absolute, this would be to be rid of all that hinders and threatens in the minds and the lives of other human beings. Of course, it would be the final tyranny.

Fortunately for human life, we are all caught up in a binding process which makes the struggle for the survival of the self an unending one. We need the wisdom and the strength of others, we need to discover the regions of the self that can be revealed to us only by the simple or complex relations that we have with others. Without them, we would not be. The tension between the *alter* and the *ego* is an abiding tension.

Nevertheless, ways must always be found for making a clearing in which one may stand in his own right. Of all the voices surrounding one, a way must be found for finding one's own voice. Despite all the bright or many-colored lights in the sky, one must be guided by the light that falls directly in one's own path. Of course, one may be mistaken, but the risk cannot be escaped if one is to achieve an authentic measure of selfhood. It is the Apostle Paul who urged his parishioners: "Let your steps be guided by such light as *you* have."

It is easy in the world to live after the world's opinion; it is easy in solitude to live after our own; but the great man is he who in the midst of the crowd keeps with perfect sweetness the independence of solitude. . . .

We Want to Be Understood

Again and again we are baffled by the confusion which we experience when we try to make clear to another what it is that our hearts would say and our minds would think. We want to be understood, to be sure that the word will be tenderly held and that the mood which is our mood will be deeply and profoundly shared. Again and again this is not our experience. We turn our eyes sometimes outward, casting a spell of judgment upon the words of others, the deeds of others, the moods of others. Sometimes when we are most ourselves, the eye turns inward and we are surprised to discover that what we did share was what we intended to share, that the searching honesty of our own hearts is something with which we ourselves are not acquainted. This is our experience with ourselves and with each other.

Waiting in the presence of God, we seek gingerly to find a way by which we may be honest—honest in our thoughts *now*, honest in our feelings *now*, honest in our desirings *now*.

We Are Visited

It is our great and blessed fortune that our lives are never left to themselves alone. We are visited in ways that we can understand and in ways that are beyond our understanding, by highlights, great moments of inspiration, quiet reassurances of grace, simple manifestations of gratuitous expressions of the goodness of life. These quiet things enrich the common life and give to the ordinary experiences of our daily grind a significance and a strength that steady and inspire. We are also surrounded by the witness of those others whose strivings have made possible so much upon which we draw from the common reservoir of our heritage, those who have carried the light against the darkness, those who have persevered when to persevere seemed idiotic and suicidal, those who have forgotten themselves in the full and creative response to something that calls them beyond the furthest reaches of their dreams and their hopes.

We are surrounded also by the witness of the life of the spirit in peculiar ways that speak directly to our hearts and to our needs: those men and women with whom in our moments of depression and despair and in our moments of joy and delight, we identify.

We are grateful to Thee, our Father, for all of the springs of joy and renewal and recreation that are our common heritage and our common lot. We offer in thanksgiving to Thee the fruits of our little lives, that they may in turn be to others a source of strength and inspiration, that apart from us they may not find fulfillment and apart from them we may not know ourselves.

We thank Thee, our Father, for so holy a privilege and we offer our thanksgiving, our dedication, and our response, not only to Thee, but to the life which is ours.

"Magic All Around Us"

> . . . There's magic all around us
> In rocks and trees, and in the minds of men,
> Deep hidden springs of magic.
> He who strikes
> the rock aright, may find them where he will.*

It is very easy to assume an attitude of indifference toward the ordinary commonplace aspects of life. This is natural because constant exposure to experiences tends to deaden one's sensitiveness to their meaning. Life does grow dingy on one's sleeve unless there is a constant awareness of the growing edge of one's experience. The mood of arrogance toward the ordinary person and the tendency to grovel in the presence of the high and powerful beset us all. This is due to the deep quest of the human spirit for status, for position, for security-rating.

I remember once meeting a most extraordinary man on a certain college campus where I was giving a series of lectures in religion. Each morning he sat in the front seat. He was a cripple—he walked suspended between two huge crutches. At the close of the last lecture, he came up to me. "Mr. Thurman, you have been very kind to me during this week. I want to give you something. Will you come to my room this evening when you are through with your work?" It was agreed.

In the interval I asked one of the students about him. He was an old fellow who earned his living by repairing shoes in a shop on top of the hill. Some of the students referred to him simply as "Old Crip."

When I entered his room in the late evening, he was standing behind a chair supporting himself very deftly. "Mr. Thurman, do you like Shakespeare? What is your favorite play?" "*Macbeth*," I replied. Then, without further ado, he read for me from memory the entire first act of *Macbeth*. And at my dictation, for over an hour, he read scene after scene from Shakespearean tragedies.

He was an old crippled man earning his living by repairing shoes for

* From the book *Watchers of the Sky* by Alfred Noyes. Copyright 1922 by J. B. Lippincott Company. Renewal 1950 by Alfred Noyes. Reprinted by permission of J. B. Lippincott Company and Hugh Noyes.

college men who thought nothing of him. There is magic all around us. It may be that the person with whom you live every day or with whom you work has, locked deep within, the answer to your own greatest need if you know how to "strike the rock aright."

The Experience of Love

There is a steady anxiety that surrounds man's experience of love. Sometimes the radiance of love is so soft and gentle that the individual sees himself with all harsh lines wiped away and all limitations blended with his strengths in so happy a combination that strength seems to be everywhere and weakness is nowhere to be found. This is a part of the magic, the spell of love. Sometimes the radiance of love kindles old fires that have long since grown cold from the neglect of despair, or new fires are kindled by a hope born full-blown without beginning and without ending. Sometimes the radiance of love blesses a life with a vision of its possibilities never before dreamed of or sought, stimulating new endeavor and summoning all latent powers to energize the life at its inmost core.

But there are other ways by which love works its perfect work. It may stab the spirit by calling forth a bitter, scathing self-judgment. The heights to which it calls may seem so high that all incentive is lost and the individual is stricken with an utter hopelessness and despair. It may throw in relief old and forgotten weaknesses to which one has made the adjustment of acceptance—but which now stir in their place to offer themselves as testimony of one's unworthiness and to challenge the love with their embarrassing authenticity. It is at such times that one expects love to be dimmed under the mistaken notion that love is at long last based upon merit and worth.

Behold the miracle! Love has no awareness of merit or demerit; it has no scale by which its portion may be weighed or measured. It does not seek to balance giving and receiving. Love loves; this is its nature. But this does not mean that love is blind, naïve, or pretentious. It does mean that love holds its object securely in its grasp, calling all that it sees by its true name but surrounding all with a wisdom born both of its passion and its understanding. Here is no traffic in sentimentality, no catering to weakness or to strength. Instead, there is robust vitality that quickens the roots of personality, creating an unfolding of the self that redefines, reshapes, and makes all things new. Such an experience is so fundamental in quality that an individual knows that what is happening to him can outlast all things without itself being dissipated or lost.

Whence comes this power which seems to be the point of referral for all experience and the essence of all meaning? No created thing, no single unit of life, can be the source of such fullness and completeness. For in the experience itself a man is caught and held by something so much more than he can ever think or be that there is but one word by which its meaning can be encompassed—God. Hence the Psalmist says that as long as the love of God shines on us undimmed, not only may no darkness obscure but also we may find our way to a point in other hearts beyond all weakness and all strength, beyond all that is good and beyond all that is evil. There is nothing outside ourselves, no circumstance, no condition, no vicissitude, that can ultimately separate us from the love of God and from the love of one another. And we pour out our gratitude to God that this is so!

Let Us Remember the Children

There is a strange power inherent in the spirit of man. Sitting or standing or lying in one place, he can bring before his presence those long separated from him by distance or by death, those whose plight he understands but whose faces he has never seen and whose names register in him no meaning.

Let us bring before our spirits the children of the world! The children born in refugee camps where all is tentative and shadowy, except the hardness of the constant anguish and anxiety that have settled deep within the eyes of those who answer when the call is "Mommy" or "Daddy" . . . the numberless host of orphans corralled like sheep in places of refuge where the common conscience provides bread to eat, water to drink, and clothes to cover the nakedness and the shame . . . the inarticulate groan of those who are the offspring of hot lust held in its place by exploding shells and the insanity of war— these are the special wards of the collective guilt of the human race, the brood left behind when armies moved and the strategy of war made towns into a desolation.

The illegitimate children of peacetime, who have no peg upon which to hang the identity of meaning, whose tender lives are cut adrift from all harbors of refuge and security—these are choked by a shame not of their making and who look upon their own existence with heartache and humiliation.

The children in families where all love is perishing and they cannot even sense the awareness that their own lives are touched by love's gentleness and strength.

The sick children who were ushered into the world as if their bodies were maimed and twisted by disaster which was their lot in some encounter before the fullness of time gave them birth among the children of men. Those who played and romped on the hillside but now will never walk again. Those who once enjoyed the beauty of sky and earth, who looked upon everything about them with unsullied wonder, but who are closed in darkness never to see again. The children of the halting, stumbling mind in whom some precious ingredient is lacking, leaving in its place the vacant mindless stare. The children of great and good fortune whose lives have been always surrounded by the tenderness of affection and the gentleness of under- standing, across whose paths no shadows have fallen and for whom life is beautiful and free—

What we bring before our presence, our Father, we share with Thee in our time of quiet prayer. We thank Thee for the gift to do this, the strange power inherent in our spirits. Grant that what we see in this way may not leave us untouched but may inspire us to be active, responsive instruments in Thy hands to heal Thy children, to bless Thy children, to redeem Thy children.

The Sacrament of Remembrance

For us this is a moment of recollection—a sacrament of remem- brance. We bring before our minds and our spirits, supported by the sureness of our feeling, those whom we love deeply, and their needs: those who are sick of body or tormented of mind; those who are now, this moment, wrestling with great and eager temptation, who fail again and again and again; those whom we love but find it, oh, so hard to like; those whom we love but find it, oh, so hard to trust. We bring them, each one of them, before our own minds, and we tarry in and with their spirits.

We remember the little children. We call to mind those whom we have had and lost; those whom we have longed to have but never had; those whom we can never have and whose lives will never bless our own because for us the time, the season, has passed. All the children of the world: those we know well and intimately; those whose stories have crept into our minds through word of mouth or through devious ways—the hungry children, the destitute children, the starving, frightened, scarred, bedraggled children; we bring quietly and sensitively before our minds and spirits, all children.

We remember the old and the aging: those who have banked their fires long since and are waiting in the wings for the final shuffle across the stage; those who have been deserted and left in their solitariness, their loneliness, even their memories shattered. We bring before our minds and spirits the old and the aging.

Our Father, we are burdened with our recollections and we struggle beneath the weight of our memories. We seek how we may offer all to Thee in the quietness of our own inward parts, in the silence of this place. Brood over ourselves and our recollections with Thy spirit until at last there may grow up within us insight, wisdom, and new levels of sensitiveness that we may be redemptive in all that we do this day and beyond. Our need, O God, is great!

Our Children Are Not *Things*

It is in order to think about children and our relationship to them. Often we underestimate both our influence and our responsibility with reference to children because they do not seem to be mindful of our presence except in terms of something to resist. The world of the adult is in some ways a different world from that of the child. We bring to bear upon life the cumulative judgment garnered from our years of living, of trial and error, of many, many discoveries along the way. It is from that kind of context that we judge the behavior of children.

But they have not lived and there is much that can be known and understood only from the harvest of the years. This fact should not blind us to the profound way in which we determine even in detail the attitudes and the very structure of the child's thought. If we are good to the child and to other people, he will get from us directly a conception of goodness more profound and significant than all the words we may use about goodness as an ideal. If we lose our temper and give way to hard, brittle words which we fling around and about, the child learns more profoundly and significantly than all the formal teaching about self-control which may be offered him.

If we love a child, and the child senses from our relationship with others that we love them, he will get a concept of love that all the subsequent hatred in the world will never be quite able to destroy. It is idle to teach the child formally about respect for other people or other groups if in little ways we demonstrate that we have no authentic respect for other people and other groups. The feeling tone and insight of the child are apt to be unerring. It is not important whether the child is able to comprehend the words we use or understand the ideas that we make articulate. The child draws his *meaning* from the meaning which we put into things that we do and say. Let us not be deceived.

We may incorporate in our formal planning all kinds of ideas for the benefit of the children. We may provide them with tools of various kinds. But if there is not genuineness in our climate, if in little ways we regard them as nuisances, as irritations, as *things* in the way of our pursuits, they will know that we do not love them and that our religion has no contagion for them. Let us gather around our children and give to them the security that can come only from associating with adults who mean what they say and who share in deeds which are broadcast in words.

Twilights and Endless Landscapes

The intimate and gentle blanket of twilight had covered the desert with a softness highlighted by the restrained radiance of the disappearing sun. All the fears of war, the terrible bitterness of the market place, the deep insecurities of modern life, seemed far removed from the surrounding quiet.

Long before the coming of cities, long before the coming of men, there were twilights, radiant and glowing skies and endless landscapes. It may be that long after the earth has reclaimed the cities and the last traces of man's fevered life have been gathered into the Great Quiet, there will be twilights, radiant and glowing skies and endless landscapes.

It is not because man and his cities are not significant that they cannot outlast the twilights, the radiant and glowing skies, and the endless landscapes. But their significance is of another kind. Man and his cities spring out of the earth; they are the children of the Great Womb that breathes through twilights, radiant and glowing skies and endless landscapes. Man and his cities, caught in the web their dreams inspire, manage to push the twilights out of mind. They wear themselves out and they forget from whence they come and in what, at long last, they find their strength. Their dreams become nightmares, their hopes become fears, and the same story repeats itself; they are claimed in the end by the twilights, the radiant and glowing skies and endless landscapes.

The more hectic the life of the cities, the more greedy and lustful the heart and mind of man, the more he forgets the meaning of the twilights, the radiant and glowing skies and endless landscapes. It is not too late. Man and his cities may yet be saved. There is still time to remember that there is twilight, the creative isthmus joining day with night. It is the time of pause when nature changes her guard. It is the lung of time by which the rhythmic respiration of day and night is guaranteed and sustained. All living things would fade and die from too much light or too much darkness, if twilight were not. In the midst of all the madness of the present hour, twilights remain and shall settle down upon the world at the close of day and usher in the nights in endless succession, despite bombs, rockets, and flying death. This is good to remember.

Even though they look down upon the ruin of cities and the fall of man, radiant and glowing skies will still trumpet their glory to the God of Life. Death and destruction cannot permanently obscure their wonder or drown their song. To remember this is to safeguard each day with the margin of strength that invades the soul from the radiant and glowing skies. These declare the glory and the tenderness of God.

To Be Secure

What if the sky falls,
The earth quakes,
The mountain turns upside down,
The swelling sea dries up,
And the sun comes down,
To one who has attained the perfect Lord?

These words from a seventh-century Tamil poet give expression to the ultimate basis of certainty in the midst of the shifting scenes of human experience. The inference is that under normal circumstances, man establishes his sense of certainty and permanence by the presence of these qualities in the external world of nature. Always there is the sky; though there be comets, shooting stars, eclipses, lowering clouds, the sky remains with, in, and beyond all the activities in the heavens. It is difficult to measure the significance of this fact in inspiring confidence in the generations of men. The earth is regarded as sure and solid. Even the phrase "terra firma" carries the meaning of the substantial, stable earth underfoot. This is one of the reasons why an earthquake is basically terrifying. The very citadel of certainty of place, moment, and position is undermined in the moment when the too too solid earth shifts and shakes.

How often in the long story of man on the planet have poets and singers appealed to the mountains for reassurance and for confidence. Each of us responds to the Psalmist, "I will lift up mine eyes unto the hills." If the mountains were turned upside down, it is difficult to structure the acute desperation that would grip the spirit of man. And the sea—the source and the goal of all the waters of all the land. The sea is—ships may go down, the earth itself may shift and lose its boundaries, but the oceans continue to ebb and flow and the fears come and go. If the sea dried up—the thought is too terrible to contemplate. The poet insists, however, that if all these things happen, the spirit of the man who has found deep within himself the dwelling place of God, would be secure. Why! Because certainty, assurance, is a quality of being and not in the materials of the context in which one may be living, regardless of their stability. Only such a person can abide all of experience and look out upon life with quiet eyes.

Joy Is of Many Kinds

Joy is of many kinds. Sometimes it comes silently, opening all closed doors and making itself at home in the desolate heart. It has no forerunner save itself; it brings its own welcome and salutation.

Sometimes joy is compounded of many elements: a touch of sadness, a whimper of pain, a harsh word tenderly held until all its arrogance dies, the casting of the eye into the face that understands, the clasp of a hand that holds, then releases, a murmur of tenderness where no word is spoken, the distilled moment of remembrance of a day, a night, an hour, lived beyond the sweep of the daily round—joy is often compounded of many things.

There is earned joy: an impossible job tackled and conquered, leaving no energy for assessing the price or measuring the cost, only an all-inclusive sense of well-being in the mind, and slowly creeping through all the crevices of the spirit—or it may be some dread has reared its head, gathering into itself all hope that is unassigned, until it becomes the master of the house, then relief comes through fresh knowledge, new insight, clearer vision. What was dread, now proves groundless and the heart takes to wings like an eagle in its flight.

There is the joy that is given. There are those who have in themselves the gift of Joy. It has no relation to merit or demerit. It is not a quality they have wrested from the vicissitudes of life. Such people have not fought and won a hard battle; they have made no conquest. To them Joy is given as a precious ingredient in life. Wherever they go, they give birth to Joy in others—they are the heavenly troubadours, earthbound, who spread their music all around and who sing their song without words and without sounds. To be touched by them is to be blessed of God. They give even as they have been given. Their presence is a benediction and a grace. In them we hear the music in the score and in their faces we sense a glory which is the very light of heaven.

Moments of Complete Joy

Whether your childhood was sad or happy as you look back upon it, there is one thing about it that is true. There were moments of intense and complete joy, which for the instant left nothing to be desired. It may have been your first new dress, or new suit; the thing about which you had dreamed for, oh, so many days was actually yours! Perhaps it was the first time you received a letter through the mail; your name was actually written on the envelope and it had come through the mail; yes, the postman actually brought it. It may have been your first time to visit a circus to see live tigers, lions, elephants, and big, big snakes; and there was the merry-go-round and the fluffy candy and the cold pink lemonade.

Perhaps it was the time when your mother let you mix the dough for the bread or sent you on your first errand in the next block alone. You may have been eavesdropping when the teacher came to call and you heard her say how smart you were and what a joy you were to teach. (And you wondered whether your mother would remember to tell your daddy what the teacher had said. At supper you managed to bring it up, so that your mother would be reminded.)

Your greatest moment of fullness may have come when, for the first time, you were conscious that your mother loved you—that swirling sense of sheer ecstasy when you were completely aware of another's love. Do you remember? It was a foretaste of something for which you would be in quest all the rest of your days: the matured relationships of friends and loved ones, of husband and wife; and that gradual or climactic moment of religious fulfillment when the heart and mind echo the words of Augustine: "Thou hast made us for Thyself and our souls are restless till they find their rest in Thee!"

Your Joy

What is the source of your joy?

There are some who are dependent upon the mood of others for their happiness. They seem bound in mood one to another like Siamese twins. If the other person is happy, the happiness is immediately contagious. If the other person is sad, there is no insulation against his mood.

There are some whose joy is dependent upon circumstances. When things do not go well, a deep gloom settles upon them, and all who touch their lives are caught in the fog of their despair. There are some whose joy is a matter of disposition and temperament. They cannot be sad because their glands will not let them. Their joy is not a matter for congratulations or praise; it is a gift of life, a talent, a gratuitous offering placed in their organism.

There are some who must win their joy against high odds, squeeze it out of the arid ground of their living, or wrest it from the stubborn sadness of circumstance. It is a determined joy, sharpened by the zest of triumph.

There are still others who find their joy deep in the heart of their religious experience. It is not related to, dependent upon, or derived from, any circumstances or conditions in the midst of which they must live. It is a joy independent of all vicissitudes. There is a strange quality of awe in their joy that is but a reflection of the deep calm water of the spirit out of which it comes. It is primarily a discovery of the soul, when God makes known His presence, where there are no words, no outward song, only the Divine Movement. This is the joy that the world cannot give. This is the joy that keeps watch against all the emissaries of sadness of mind and weariness of soul. This is the joy that comforts and is the companion, as we walk even through the valley of the shadow of death.

"To Him That Waits"

To him that waits, all things reveal themselves, provided that he has the courage not to deny in the darkness what he has seen in the light.

Waiting is a window opening on many landscapes. For some, waiting means the cessation of all activity when energy is gone and exhaustion is all that the heart can manage. It is the long slow panting of the spirit. There is no will to will—"spent" is the word. There is no hope, not hopelessness—there is no sense of anticipation or even awareness of a loss of hope. Perhaps even the memory of function itself has faded. There is now and before—there is no after.

For some, waiting is a time of intense preparation for the next leg of the journey. Here at last comes a moment when forces can be realigned and a new attack upon an old problem can be set in order. Or it may be a time of reassessment of all plans and of checking past failures against present insight. It may be the moment of the long look ahead when the landscape stretches far in many directions and the chance to select one's way among many choices cannot be denied.

For some, waiting is a sense of disaster of the soul. It is what Francis Thompson suggests in the line: "Naked I wait Thy love's uplifted stroke!" The last hiding place has been abandoned because even the idea of escape is without meaning. Here is no fear, no panic, only the sheer excruciation of utter disaster. It is a kind of emotional blackout in the final moment before the crash—it is the passage through the Zone of Treacherous Quiet.

For many, waiting is something more than all of this. It is the experience of recovering balance when catapulted from one's place. It is the quiet forming of a pattern of recollection in which there is called into focus the fragmentary values from myriad encounters of many kinds in a lifetime of living. It is to watch a gathering darkness until all light is swallowed up completely without the power to interfere or bring a halt. Then to continue one's journey in the darkness with one's footsteps guided by the illumination of remembered radiance is to know courage of a peculiar kind—the courage to demand that light continue to be light even in the surrounding darkness. To walk in the light while darkness invades, envelops, and surrounds is to wait on the Lord. This is to know the renewal of strength. This is to walk and faint not.

Your Loneliness

What do you do with your loneliness? One of the massive results of the invasion of privacy so characteristic of our times is the increasing fear of being alone.

Loneliness is of many kinds. There is the loneliness of a great bitterness when the pain is so great that any contact with others threatens to open old wounds and to awaken old frenzies. There is the loneliness of the broken heart and the dead friendship, when what was full of promise and fulfillment lost its way in a fog of misunderstanding, anxiety, and fear. There is the loneliness of those who have absorbed so much of violence that all hurt has died, leaving only the charred reminder of a lost awareness. There is the loneliness of the shy and the retiring where timidity stands guard against all encounters and the will to relate to others is stilled. There is the loneliness of despair, the exhaustion of the spirit, leaving no strength to try again; the promise of the second wind can find no backing. There is the loneliness of death when silently a man listens, one by one, to the closing of all doors, and all that remains is naked life, stripped of everything that shields, protects, and insulates.

But there is loneliness in another key. There is the loneliness of the truth-seeker whose search swings him out beyond all frontiers and all boundaries, until there bursts upon his view a fleeting moment of utter awareness and he *knows* beyond all doubt, all contradictions. There is the loneliness of the moment of integrity when the declaration of the self is demanded and the commitment gives no corner to sham, to pretense, or to lying. There is the loneliness in the moment of creation when the new comes into being, trembles, then steadies and finds its way. There is the loneliness of those who walk with God until the path takes them out beyond all creeds and all faiths and they know the wholeness of communion and the bliss of finally being understood.

Loneliness is of many kinds. What do you do with yours?

"The Night View of the World"

"Upon the night view of the world, a day view must follow." This is an ancient insight grounded in the experience of the race in its long journey through all the years of man's becoming. Here is no cold idea born out of the vigil of some solitary thinker in lonely retreat from the traffic of the common ways. It is not the wisdom of the book put down in ordered words by the learned and the schooled. It is insight woven into the pattern of all living things, reaching its grand apotheosis in the reflection of man gazing deep into the heart of his own experience.

That the day view follows the night view is written large in nature. Indeed it is one with nature itself. The clouds gather heavy with unshed tears; at last they burst, sending over the total landscape waters gathered from the silent offering of sea and river. The next day dawns and the whole heavens are aflame with the glorious brilliance of the sun. This is the way the rhythm moves. The fall of the year comes, then winter with its trees stripped of leaf and bud; cold winds ruthless in bitterness and sting. One day there is sleet and ice; in the silence of the nighttime the snow falls soundlessly—all this until at last the cold seems endless and all there is seems to be shadowy and foreboding. The earth is weary and heavy. Then something stirs—a strange new vitality pulses through everything. One can feel the pressure of some vast energy pushing, always pushing through dead branches, slumbering roots—life surges everywhere within and without. Spring has come. The day usurps the night view.

Is there any wonder that deeper than idea and concept is the insistent conviction that the night can never stay, that winter is ever moving toward the spring? Thus, when a man sees the lights go out one by one, when he sees the end of his days marked by death— his death—he *senses*, rather than knows, that even the night into which he is entering will be followed by day. It remains for religion to give this ancient wisdom phrase and symbol. For millions of men and women in many climes this phrase and this symbol are forever one with Jesus, the Prophet from Galilee. When the preacher says as a part of the last rites, "I am the Resurrection and the Life, . . ." he is reminding us all of the ancient wisdom: "Upon the night view of the world, a day view must follow."

The Miracle of Living

Frequently we are filled with a strange sense of the mystery and the miracle of life. In our private lives we are mindful of many blessings in a minor key, blessings so intimate, so closely binding, that they do not seem to be blessings at all:

The ability to get tired and to be renewed by rest and relaxation; the whole range of tastes from sweet to bitter and the subtleties in between; the peculiar quality that cool water has for quenching the thirst; the color of sky and sea and the vast complex of hues that blend with objects, making the eye the inlet from rivers of movement and form; the sheer wonder of sound that gives to the inward parts feeling tones of the heights and the depths; the tender remembrance of moments that were good and whole, of places that reached out and claimed one as their very own, of persons who shared at depths beyond all measuring; the coming of day and the sureness of the return of the night, and all the dimensions of meaning that each of us finds in this cycle of movement which sustains and holds fast in the security of its rhythms. Thus, in our private lives, we are mindful of many blessings in a minor key.

Then there are the vast and lumbering awarenesses that live in us for which our hearts sing their joyful "amen":

The land of our birth—the quality of climate that does not undermine the natural strength of body, the technique and skill by which we are able to secure the windbreak against wind and storm, rain and heat; the fact and experience of family life where all the ingredients of the good life may first be made our own, against the time when we make our own way after the pattern of our own need for understanding.

Beyond all these there is the intimate sense of being upheld and cradled by strength that is not of our making, something that gives to life a quality of integrity and meaning which we, of ourselves, could never generate; the gentle upheaval in the heart reminding us to lift up our heads and be of good courage—

All of the benedictions of life flow in upon us, our Father—teach us how to make of our lives a Sacrament in Thy Hand, lest our spirits die and we vanish as shadows in the night.

"A Gracious Spirit"

I seek this day a gracious spirit.

I seek a gracious spirit in dealing with my own conflicts. It is often easy for me to be extremely hard on myself. Often I tend to give myself the disadvantage and to wallow in blame and condemnation as distinguished from self-pity. It is a part of my pretense to be gracious in my spirit in dealing with conflicts at the point in which others are involved, but not with myself. Is this really true, or is it just the reverse? Do I dare expose all of my intent to the scrutiny of God? Dare I seek the understanding of God and His wisdom in facing my own conflict? Again and again, I am aware that the Light not only illumines but it also *burns*.

I seek a gracious spirit in dealing with the injustices of the world. This I do not confuse with softness, or fear, or cowardice, or sentimentality. I must know clearly the evilness of evil and recognize it for what it is—stark, brutal, terrifying. I must oppose it, place the full weight of whatever forces I have thoroughly against it. At the same time, I cannot escape the fact that every judgment is a self-judgment, that even as I resist evil I share the guilt of evil. It is this sense of sharing the guilt of evil that should inspire the gracious spirit in dealing with injustice. I do not want to admit even before God the necessity for this spirit. I fear that it will make me soft and weak. It is out of the depths of my own imperfections that I dare seek the gracious spirit as I wait in the presence of God this day.

I seek this day a gracious spirit.

Teach Me Thy Grace

Teach me Thy Grace in all the little things of life.

My days are surrounded by myriad little things. There are the little words of every day: simple greetings, yes and no, commonplace expressions of courtesy, minor services of daily routine. There are many little tastes: bread, milk, tea, coffee, salt, sugar, meat, all blended to satisfy hunger and to meet bodily demand. There are little deeds of unasked-for kindness: a button sewed on, a shared personal delight, a gentle reminder of something that had slipped out of mind. Teach me Thy Grace in all the little things of life.

Teach me Thy Grace in the daily work by which I earn my keep and the keep of those dependent upon me.

There are duties demanded of me that irk and irritate, dulling the cutting edge of joy in labor. There is the fatigue that burrows deep into the citadel of my sense of well-being, rendering me brittle, sharp in speech, and short in patience. There is the pride, the arrogance that comes when I turn my eyes from the high level of my intent and look coldly at the lesser deeds of some who walk the way with me. There is the tendency to wrap myself in garments of my own compassion ending in the muck of self-pity and unhealthy moodiness.

Teach me Thy Grace in the daily work by which I earn my keep and the keep of those dependent upon me.

Teach me Thy Grace.

A Prayer for Peace

Our Father, fresh from the world with the smell of life upon us, we make an act of prayer in the silence of this place. Our minds are troubled because the anxieties of our hearts are deep and searching.

We are stifled by the odor of death which envelops the earth because in so many places brother fights against brother. The panic of fear, the torture of insecurity, the ache of hunger—all have fed and rekindled ancient hatreds and long-forgotten memories of old struggles when the world was young and Thy children were but dimly aware of Thy Presence in the midst. For all this we seek forgiveness. There is no one of us without guilt, and before Thee we confess our sins: we are proud and arrogant; we are selfish and greedy; we have harbored in our hearts and minds much that makes for bitterness, hatred, and revenge.

While we wait in Thy Presence, search our spirits and grant to our minds the guidance and the wisdom that will teach us the way to take, without which there can be no peace and no confidence anywhere. Teach us how to put at the disposal of Thy Purposes of Peace the fruits of our industry, the products of our minds, the vast wealth of our land, and the resources of our spirit. Grant unto us the courage to follow the illumination of this hour, to the end that we shall not lead death to any man's door, but rather may we strengthen the hands of all in high places and in common tasks who seek to build a friendly world of friendly men, beneath a friendly sky. This is the simple desire of our hearts which we share with Thee in quiet confidence.

We Behold Our Lives

Our Father, we have turned aside from the paths, the duties, and the responsibilities which involve us day after day, to feel ourselves into Thy Presence with as much confidence and faith as we can muster. It is our simple trust that before Thee in the great quietness of this waiting moment we may find the measure of deep and central peace without which the enterprises of our private life cannot be fulfilled. We spread before Thee all the meaning that we have been able to garner out of the days of our living.

We see, as if by a flash of blinding light, the meaning of some things we have done since last we talked with Thee: the hasty word, the careless utterance, the deliberate act by which another was injured or confused, the decision to do what even at the time of the decision we knew was neither the right thing nor the thing we were willing to back with our lives. All of these things push their way to the center of our thought, our Father, that we may be exercised in sincerity, uttering before Thee what is honest and clear.

Sitting in the midst of so much within us that is not good even by our paltry standards, there begins to stir, as a great burning in our depths, the vast urgency for forgiveness. Forgiveness, our Father; forgiveness for the sin, forgiveness for the wrong act, forgiveness for the bad deed.

We do not know altogether what it is we need beyond this. We see our lives, the goals which we have set for ourselves. These goals, these dreams, are weighted and held in tender balance before Thy scrutiny and Thy caring—we see them now in a new light, in a fresh way. We trust that somehow, as we move into the tasks that await us, the radiance which we sense now will cast a long glow to guide us in tomorrow's darkness.

We are mindful of needs beyond our little world and its demands. Some needs close at hand have not been able to get beyond the outer gate of our vital concern—we have dealt with them casually out of the richness of our own sense of surplus. There are those other needs at which we have not dared to look, because we fear what our response to them would make us do or make us become. They might upset all the careful plans of our days, and the goals upon which we have set our spirits may be thrown out of focus or cast aside. O God, we cannot look into the depths of certain anguish and find our way into our own happiness again. This seems too costly for us and we are afraid. And yet, our Father, as we are stilled before Thee, these needs move before us, we hear the cry and the anguish of the destitute, of the hungry, of the hopeless, the despairing, and we cannot be deaf. But we do not know what to do. We do not know *how* to give, and not destroy ourselves.

Gentle Father, deal with our disorder with redemptive tenderness so that we, as we live, tomorrow and tomorrow, may not be shamed by Thy Grace that has made our lives move in such tranquil places. These are all the words we have; take them and permit them to say to Thee the content of our hearts and our spirits. Merciful God, Merciful God . . .

The Ceiling of Thy Hopes
I Will Lift on High

The Ceiling of Thy Hopes: it is easier to believe *little* than to believe *big*. The immediate demand is often so urgent, the immediate problem is often so acute or so insoluble, that the ceiling of hope is lowered, leaving but little room even for breathing. Sometimes the ordinary routines spread over all one's working hours like morning dew, and one seeks in vain for a free margin, for the deep breath, the long look, the heartening gaze. At such a moment, life seems not only to close in around us but it also seems to close down upon us.

I will lift on high the ceiling of thy hopes. This is the promise of renewal, the spoken word of faith as literal fact. How does God accomplish this? How is the ceiling lifted? It may be lifted by a sudden or a slow shift in the pattern of the days. There may be unforeseen changes or premeditated rearrangements which place one on top of, rather than underneath, his load. Sometimes the change is accomplished by making a new relationship with other human beings, and out of it emerges the contagion of heightened hopes. But most often God may effect the miracle by a quiet release of fresh energy deep within the spirit which pushes the ceiling of one's hope higher and higher.

The deep breath, the long look, the heartening gaze—when did they come? One may not know. He knows only that a change has taken place, something has happened; things are not seen as being what they once were. Let us rejoice and with thanksgiving, that the ceiling of our hopes God will lift on high.

To be sustained by such a confidence is to look out on life with quiet eyes.

A Prayer of Old Age

Age is a matter of perspective, attitude, and digestion. There are many people who are young in years but are old in reactions, who have lost their resiliency and are already exhausted.—Others who are full of years, chronologically, but continue to be alert, sensitive, and elastic. For most people, it is difficult to accept the fact of increasing years.

The human body tends to prepare the mind for old age by providing the basis for a kind of covering philosophy. When a sixty-year-old person sees someone half his age leaping up the stairs four at a time, he says to himself, "How stupid to wear yourself out in needless exertion!" All of us must accommodate ourselves to the simple fact that we are not so young as we once were, and thus take life in the stride belonging to the years we have lived.

A friend of mine gave me, the other day, a copy of a prayer written by a lady past ninety years of age. Her whole life had been spent in Elyria, Ohio. This is her prayer:

O God, our Heavenly Father, whose gift is length of days, help us to make the noblest use of mind and body in our advancing years. According to our strength, apportion Thou our work. As Thou has pardoned our transgressions, sift the ingatherings of our memory, that evil may grow dim and good may shine forth clearly. We bless Thee for Thy gifts and especially for Thy presence and the love of friends in heaven and on earth. Grant us new ties of friendship, new opportunities of service, joy in the growth and happiness of children, sympathy with those who bear the burdens of the world, clear thought, and quiet faith. Teach us to bear infirmities with cheerful patience. Keep us from narrow pride in outgrown ways, blind eyes that will not see the good of change, impatient judgments of the methods and experiments of others. Let Thy peace rule our spirits through all the trials of our waning powers. Take from us all fear of death, and all despair, and undue love of life; that, with glad hearts at rest in Thee, we may await Thy will concerning us, through Jesus Christ our Lord.

A New Melody

The old song of my spirit has wearied itself out. It has long ago been learned by heart so that now it repeats itself over and over, bringing no added joy to my days or lift to my spirit. It is a good song, measured to a rhythm to which I am bound by ties of habit and timidity of mind. The words belong to old experiences which once sprang fresh as water from a mountain crevice fed by melting snows. But my life has passed beyond to other levels where the old song is meaningless. I demand of the old song that it meet the need of present urgencies. Also, I know that the work of the old song, perfect in its place, is not for the new demand!

I will sing a new song. As difficult as it is, I must learn the new song that is capable of meeting the new need. I must fashion new words born of all the new growth of my life, my mind, and my spirit. I must prepare for new melodies that have never been mine before, that all that is within me may lift my voice unto God. How I love the old familiarity of the wearied melody—how I shrink from the harsh discords of the new untried harmonies.

Teach me, my Father, that I might learn with the abandonment and enthusiasm of Jesus, the fresh new accent, the untried melody, to meet the need of the untried morrow. Thus, I may rejoice with each new day and delight my spirit in *each fresh* unfolding.

I will sing, this day, a new song unto Thee, O God.

The Common Mood

It is a very blessed thing to be privileged to share together the common mood, the full and searching moment in which the meaning of the private life is lifted up and seen in a perspective as broad as life and as profound. Again and again we are overwhelmed by the littleness of our lives, the way in which there seems to close in upon us the intimate need, the personal demand. No breathing moment permits us to lift up our heads and take the long look and sense ultimate meanings in which our lives are involved.

Thus each has his world of need and necessity and urgency; some of us are wrestling with very great anxieties. We do not know how to deal with that which awaits us tomorrow, and in our desperation and our panic we find ourselves unable to center our spirits upon the meaning of this great and significant moment in our lives.

There are some who are ill and we have no way to determine now what this illness says about the length of our lives. We wrestle with this secondary undertone of uneasiness while we await the revelation of the trained mind and the skilled hand.

There are some who are deeply troubled about the state of the world—the fever that seems to be sending our civilization hurtling along a path which threatens to end in destruction and carnage and great tragic waste.

Thus we clutch this moment of intimacy and friendliness and put it over against all the darkness that seems to be brooding over the nations of the world. There are some who remember the meaning of this day in the richness and tradition of the faith, and we seek ways by which we may enter into this meaning in our own way so that there will be in us no thing that will spoil the fullness of the joy of the moment of triumph.

Here we are, our Father, all of us Thy children, each with his own life and world and need. We lay gently upon Thy altar our life as it is, and we hold it there, waiting for Thy Spirit to invade our spirits so that we shall be prepared for the living of our lives, whatever may be the circumstances by which our days, tomorrow and tomorrow, may be surrounded. For this, O God, we utter in the quietness our thanks and our praise.

Christmas

This is the season of the year when so many things stand out in stark outline against the background of our days. We think of little children all over the world; children in refugee camps who have known aught else throughout the length of their days; children in orphanages in our own land and in other lands; rootless children; children in families where there is so little love that they are unaware that their own lives are touched by its gentleness and strength; sick children, those who have walked and will never walk again, those who have looked out on the beauty of the world and will never see it again. Our hearts are touched and melt in the quietness as we remember the children of the world.

We remember the old people. Those whose fires have been banked, and who sit in their solitariness, some with minds broken by the hardness of their days, who cannot be comforted by the memories of other times; some who at this season of the year hunger and thirst for the love of their children, and find it not; some who live in homes for the aged, surrounded by those of their kind, who huddle together, hoping that in the warmth of each other's personality and spirit they might find strength sufficient for another day.

God of our hearts and our lives, accept the tenderness which we pour out in our thoughts and in our memories and desires, and grant that it will inform our deeds, so that during these days that are upon us, to the limit of our strength and beyond, we may be messengers of Thy tidings, and sharers of Thy peace.

To Rise to the Great Occasion

It is not too difficult to rise to the great occasion, to put forth the tremendous effort for the great moment. Again and again men find it possible to withstand the great temptation, to measure up to the formidable enemy who threatens or challenges.

The radical test for life seems to be most actively at work in the experience in which the stakes are highest and most exacting. This is always a part of the appeal of war. When the nation is threatened, then every man becomes important in a new way. He may not have counted before but at a time of national peril the total welfare becomes an insistent part of his responsibility. Have you ever been in a regional or city disaster caused by flood, earthquake, or fire? At such a time everybody becomes involved—the ne'er-do-well, the people beyond the tracks, the rich, the poor, the good, the bad. This is the moment of judgment and all must be present and accounted for.

But the most searching graces of life are made up of the "tiny nothings." The pulse of the daily round that keeps the living process on its way is the source of the sustaining quality of all of life. One of the strengths of character is the ability to stand fast at the level of the commonplace and the ordinary. When the big temptation has failed to destroy a man, he may succumb to the relentless pressure of the "tiny nothings" that will not let him be.

It is at the point of the "tiny nothings" that human beings break down when they seem most secure. The thousand little things which in themselves can never be pinpointed, the petty annoyances that puncture the rhythm of creative, daily companionship, the little word expressing the big meaning—these are the walls that rise quietly in the nighttime, shutting one man away from his fellows.

Our Father, greatly increase the quality of our awareness of the little processes which make up the daily round of our living. Tenderize all the hard places in our emotions that we may be alive to Thy Spirit in the simplest exposures of the daily round.

The
Great Incarnate Words

The Great Incarnate Words

The hours lay heavily upon the heart of the old man.
Years of waiting and longing had dimmed his eyes;
While before him stretched the long interminable hours
With no fulfillment.
> "How long, O Jehovah, before the Hope takes flesh,
> Before the sons of Israel may shout aloud
> A new song:
>> 'Behold, He is here!
>> The Deliverer has come at last!' "

In a quiet manger full of the animal sweat,
The healthy sounds of tired beasts,
The maiden womb of Israel's Daughter
Opened wide its flood gates, pushing into a waiting moment
The expected child!
When the old man saw what God had wrought,
His heart flung off the weight of years
To give wide sweep to urgent words:
> "Now, Lord, let thy servant depart in peace
> For mine eyes have seen . . .
> This child is the sign of man's attack."

The family was poor!
The Day of Consecration came
But the price for the Lamb of Sacrifice could not be found;
Only the doves of the poor to use.
Poverty, the watchword of the mass of men,
Marked him early as Son of Man.

The child was a Jew;
The challenge to all the funded hates of men
Who, through centuries, struggled against the imperious demand
Of an ultimate ethic:
> Men must be brothers achieved,
> As they are brothers in blood and seed.
Blessed Israel, guardian of the One-God-Dream,

The eternal sufferer whose agony is the anguished cry of all mankind,
In hectic, patient, turbulent search for
The Great Fulfillment.
He was a word made flesh!
But the word, what was it?
Not for the proud, not for the mighty,
The dominant aggressive cornerers of the groans and struggles
Of the sweating masses.

There is no future for the proud;
Only a past.
The gaze of the powerful
Must always focus on yesterday!
The word, what was it?
It was for men whose backs are against the wall;
Whose hope feeds eternally on itself, always consuming, but never
　　　consumed.

Fear not, that was the word.
Fear, the great companion of the poor,
The creeping, slinking Hound ever on the trail of the
Bedevilled seekers for surcease from oppression and wrong.
The poor know fear—
Fear of a special breed.
For them, fear is a climate closing in!
It is breathless humidity.
It clings like dampness in the air
When long hours of steady rain
Crush the days and nights with wetness.
This is not fear of death.
All men soon or late make calm their minds,
And quiet their anxious spirits before the sure
Relentless fact of Death.
This is the fear of being finally outraged by life—
Cast upon by violent hands,
Unrestrained by order of the mind or heart;
Caught in the terrible grapple of blind or
Calculating brutality, with no defense of public will or
Private conscience to avail.
To die without benefit of Cause—
　　　No great end served—
　　　No trumpet blasts—

No banners wave;
Not even the bright transcendent glow of martyr's fire;
Only the sordid overflow of passions,
Catching in their swirling churn the hopeless victims
Of a brother's scorn.
This is the final degradation;
The ultimate shame.
The weak, the poor, the dispossessed, are schooled in fear.
It presides over decisions,
Weighs all choices of the simplest kind.
It reaches into the quiet places of the fireside
And conditions the behavior of young and old alike.
It causes the body to learn by rote
Complex behavior patterns to check
Some mindless slip,
Some thoughtless move,
That will send crashing down on innocent heads
A terrible judgment!
Fear becomes the great Assurance
Against floating violence!

Jesus knew all this.
  His days were nurtured in great hostilities
  Focused upon his kind, the sons of Israel.
  There was no moment in all his years
  When he was free.
  Sometimes in lonely places, beneath burning stars,
  Wrapt in the silence of the hills . . .
  He felt eternal stirrings at his roots,
  And knew that always
  Beneath him, above, beyond, within,
  The God of life kept watch.
  This was the truth he felt;
  To make it clear, to announce
  Its clarion meaning—what greater
  Boon to man?
Strange, to know all this;
To be thus assured,
Then bow before some mighty Arrogance.
  "Fear not them who kill the body
  And after that there is nothing more
  That they can do. But fear God."

That is it—the fear of God!
          the fear of man!
Which shall it be?
The one lays bare the heart of reverence,
Pours wave after wave of healing balm
Upon the broken and forlorn;
Makes strong the failing spirit,
Renews the mind and affirms the craven will.
It frees the self of carking care,
Nourishing the life with strange new courage.
It is what the birds know as their wings
Lift them high above the plains.
It is the quiet trust glimpsed in the eyes of carefree children.
It is the blushless blossoming of roadside flowers,
Or the gliding confidence of fish through quiet or troubled waters.
It is what burns in the prophet's eyes or
Glows in the tranquil spirits of those
Who have come through great tribulations.
The fear of God, the beginning of Wisdom!
Before the altars of its searching fire
The fear of man is rank and vile!
The great Blasphemy—
The supreme Sacrilege—
The final Corrosion.
"Fear not," says Jesus,
And all the Sons of men
Echo in their hearts
The triumphant Word.

The word—*Be genuine!*
Let your words be yea, yea; nay, nay!
          All else obscures truth,
Tempting man to betray the Eternal.
What a hard word for the weak!
It brings crashing down around their heads
The great fortress of defense
Against embattled power.
Somewhere in a past forgot,
In the first moments of internecine strife,
The weak took refuge behind deception's web,
Stretching their brittle threads of guarded life
Against odds too great to meet on equal terms.

The *will to live* made all else dim.
By circuitous route, by devious means,
Weaving a pattern of false leads and feinting starts,
Life kept itself intact
And did not die.

The little birds know this:
   Feeding in meadows under sun-drenched skies,
   The shadow of the Hawk appears.
   Time stops! all else forgot,
   Conditioned feet gather dead brown grass.
   A quick somersault and all is changed.
   High above, the Hawk clears his eyes,
   Shifts his course and seeks his meal
   In other fields.
   One with grass and root, they live
   For yet another day.

Little children know this:
   When parental will looms threateningly
   To deter or interfere,
   Defiance is not wise.
   By route direct and unabashed!
   A steely web of chaste deception
   Trips and holds in firm embrace
   The parental power
   Until at last it yields to the little will
   As if it were its own.

The weak know this:
All victims of Might
Draw from this churning source—
   By the waters of Babylon they mingled tears
   With flowing streams.
   Into their midst Ezekiel came
   To comfort, soothe, make unafraid.
   Words like liquid fire gushed forth at eventide—
   Flaming words, but hidden in a vibrant code,
   Crystal clear to all with ears to hear.
   Distant Tyre, and far off Egypt named he them.
   But all the biting anger of prophetic ire
   Bespoke in deftest phrase of Babylon.

The Exiles knew and were consoled,
While Babylon kept watch, unconscious of the work the
    prophet wrought.
Who said, "I am God"?—
Poor old Hiram of struggling Tyre?
Hardly.
It was the mighty king of Babylon.
The captives knew and found fresh strength.
It is an age-old way the weak have found
To fight the strong with hidden tools.

The African slave had learned this lesson well:
The master's priest with fervid tones,
Splashed on a canvas broad and high,
The glories of another world where God would add
New comforts to the blest of earth.
The slave listened well; and deep within his soul
A melody stirred:
"Everybody talkin' 'bout Heaven ain' goin' there";
There must be two heavens—he queried.
No, for there is only one God.
"Ah!" an old man said,
"I'm having my hell now;
When death calls me I go to Heaven.
He is having his Heaven now;
When death calls him, he goes to hell."
Next day 'neath withering sun, deep in the rows of blossoming
    cotton,
He cried: "I got shoes—you got shoes
All God's chillun got shoes."
His eyes fell on all his fellows acres 'round—
"But everybody talkin' 'bout Heaven"—
His eyes held the big house for one elastic minute—
"Ain' goin' there."

But the word would not be stilled:
Let your motive be simple;
Your words, yea, yea; nay, nay.
Hypocrisy for self-defense—
Is that the sinless sin?
Does it degrade the soul at last
And sweep the raft against the hidden rocks?

Deceive, and live for yet another day!
Declare, and run the risk of sure destruction!
But why?
The Word knew:
  There is a point beyond which man cannot go,
  Without yielding his right to try again.
  To play God false to save one's skin,
  May jeopardize all there is that makes man, Man.
      "What would a man give in exchange for his soul?"
  This is the great Decision!
  Even death becomes a little thing.
  To survive with inner cleanness;
  To compromise where ground forsook can be retrieved;
  To stand unyielding when the moment comes;
This is the meaning of the Word!

Love. The word—LOVE.
Hate is the last great fortress of the weak.
The moving current of resentment flows through the channels
          of the heart,
When overarching wrong inflicts its bitter lash.
But this may pass.
The subtle thrust of implied scorn may trip the mind
To send the spirit hurtling down crazy stairs,
To land at last where clever thoughts
May find retreat.

"Who is my neighbor?"
"Is it lawful to do this or that today?"
"Why do your followers eat with hands unwashed?"
"The tribute, is it lawful to pay it?"

But Hate is something more.
A time does come when the dregs of all the piled-up scorn
Of men's contempt
Mount high to overrun the cup of great endurance;
When like a flash of light that blinds,
There bursts upon the soul, the stark alarm:
  The last substance of self-respect
    Is spilled.
Alone and desperate—
Desperate and alone—

Pitiless and scarred—
The weak stand crushed.
Something stirs—the core of bitterness!
The boundless energy of great revenge melts
The shattered feelings into one great block:
And hate is born—
Hate is the validation—
The ground of courage.
New power surges—a vast fresh cunning goads the mind.
Blind to good and evil, reckless of all consequence,
The weak strike out!
Dead dreams come to life again.
And hope is born.
Now, there is no need of fellow man;
Out of the depths of his new arousal
The cry goes forth:

      I, I am autonomous!
      I, I am independent!
      I, I am God!

The world grows dark—
The green grass fades—the flowers die—
The music of the birds is still.
Naught remains save death and ashes.
The power that saved, destroys.
All this Jesus knew,
The word—Love.

      The meaning of life, what is it?
Down through the ages the deathless words ring out—
      "Hear, O Israel, the Lord thy God is one;
      And thou shalt love the Lord thy God
      With all thy heart, mind, soul and strength;
      And thou shalt love thy neighbor as thyself."
And thy neighbor? Any man whose need of thee lays claim—
Friend and foe alike. Thou must not make division.
Thy mind, heart, soul and strength must ever search
To find the way by which the road
To all men's need of thee must go.
This is the Highway of the Lord.

The
End of the Year

End of the Year

There is something which seems utterly final about the end of the year. It means that we are one year older; this is a fact definite and inexorable. We are twelve months closer to the end of our physical time span—one year closer to death. It means that in some important ways we are taken further from, or brought closer to, the goal of our living, whatever that goal may be. It means that some crucial questions which were unanswered twelve months ago have been finally and decidedly answered, and whatever doubts there may have been about the result are completely removed; now, we know. It means that we are in fuller or lesser possession of ourselves and our powers than ever before.

During the passing of the twelve months, experiences have come into our lives which revealed certain things about ourselves which we had not suspected. Some new demand was made upon us which caused us to behave in a manner that was stranger to our established pattern of life, and we felt shocked, surprised, enraged, or delighted that such was possible for us. We met someone with whom we built the kind of relationship which opened up to us new worlds of wonder and magic, which were completely closed to us a year ago. It means that we are wiser by far than we were at year's beginning.

The circling series of events upon whose bosom we have been wafted cut away our pretensions, stripping us bare of much beneath which we have hidden even from ourselves. When we saw ourselves revealed, there was born a wisdom about life and its meaning that makes us say with all our hearts this day, that life is good, not evil. It means that we have been able to watch, as if bewitched, while the illumined finger of God pointed out a path through the surrounding darkness where no path lay; exposed to our surprised gaze a door where we were sure there was only a blank wall; revealed the strong arms and assuring voices of friends when we were sure that in our plight we were alone, utterly and starkly alone.

All of these meanings and many more counsel us that because life is dynamic and we are deeply alive, the end of the year can mean only the end of the year, not the end of life, not the end of us, not even the end of time. We turn our faces toward the year being born, with a riding hope that will carry us into the days ahead with courage and with confidence. The old year dies; the new year is being born—Long live Life!

* * *

As we come to the end of the year, we observe a kind of formality about it: a sense of the closing, one by one, of doors; a sense of fruition, or a sense of the falling of leaves, depending upon our point of view and our situation. The end of the year is the end of the year; it is not the end of time; it is not the end of man's life on the planet; it is not the end of the book; it is the end of a chapter in the book. As we look back upon the past twelve months, we are confronted with a question that belongs to all of our living: what do we do with the past, what do you do with the past? Of course, the past is in a sense given. It is. "The Moving Finger writes; and, having writ, moves on," and there isn't anything we can do about the fact of the passing of the days—they belong to the past now. And the wheels of time move forward always—backward never. The past, first of all, has to be accepted; it cannot be undone—it is. It is a part of that which cannot be relived in any effective sense.

We cannot put the past back into solution that it might crystallize itself once again in terms of days or months. We *can* relate to the past in ways that are redemptive. If there are relationships we've had in the past, these past twelve months, relationships that have not been good relationships, it is possible to recognize that they are out of line with either our intent, our purposes, our hopes, or our dreams. From this vantage point we can seek to reestablish them in terms of reconciliation and healing. In this way we can redeem the past.

We can remember the past in terms of the things that were unpleasant, we can literally use our recall in a manner structured on the side of that which is pessimistic, that which makes for the dour attitude, that which makes for the negative attitude toward life. Or, we can use our memory of the past with creative discrimination. We can lift out of the past those things that will give us reinforcement as we face the future, that will give us courage, that will lift the ceiling of our hopes as we look toward the tomorrow. Because of what we have learned from this aspect of our past, we are reinforced for the future. We can thereby let the past become something more than history: something that tutors us as we move into the new year. Now that we know this, we may heal ourselves in the light of this judgment. The past is history but the past is alive, because the past is in us.

Long live life, and if life lives long in us, may it live well as we face the New Year.

Blessings at Year's End

I remember with gratitude the fruits of the labors of others, which I have shared as a part of the normal experience of daily living.

I remember the beautiful things that I have seen, heard, and felt— some, as a result of definite seeking on my part, and many that came unheralded into my path, warming my heart and rejoicing my spirit.

I remember the moments of distress that proved to be groundless and those that taught me profoundly about the evilness of evil and the goodness of good.

I remember the new people I have met, from whom I have caught glimpses of the meaning of my own life and the true character of human dignity.

I remember the dreams that haunted me during the year, keeping me ever mindful of goals and hopes which I did not realize but from which I drew inspiration to sustain my life and keep steady my purposes.

I remember the awareness of the spirit of God that sought me out in my aloneness and gave to me a sense of assurance that undercut my despair and confirmed my life with new courage and abiding hope.

This Is a New Year

This is a New Year. The calendar says so. I note the fact by marking it so when I wish to designate the day and the year as distinguished from some other day and year. It may be that my contract says so. It is indicated clearly in the lease I signed or the agreement I attested. It is curious how much difference can be marked between two dates—December 31 and January 1.

Yet there are many things that move unchanged, paying no attention to a device like the calendar or arrangements such as contracts or leases. There is the habit pattern of an individual life. Changes in that are not noted by the calendar, even though they may be noted *on* the calendar. Such changes are noted by events that make for radical shifts in values or the basic rearrangement of purposes. There are desires of the heart or moods of the spirit that may flow continuously for me whatever year the calendar indicates. The lonely heart, the joyful spirit, the churning anxiety may remain unrelieved, though the days come and go without end.

But, for many, this will be a New Year. It may mark the end of relationships of many years' accumulation. It may mean the first encounter with stark tragedy or radical illness or the first quaffing of the cup of bitterness. It may mean the great discovery of the riches of another human heart and the revelation of the secret beauty of one's own. It may mean the beginning of a new kind of living because of marriage, of graduation, of one's first job. It may mean an encounter with God on the lonely road or the hearing of one's name called by Him, high above the noise and din of the surrounding traffic. And when the call is answered, the life becomes invaded by smiling energies never before released, felt, or experienced. In whatever sense this year is a New Year for you, may the moment find you eager and unafraid, ready to take it by the hand with joy and with gratitude.

The New Year

I

There is always something impressive about a fresh start. Think how fortunate it would be if time was not somehow divided into parts. Suppose there were no day, only night. Even in parts of the world near the North Pole, there is a six-month day and a six-month night. Or suppose there were only winter, or only summer, or only spring. Suppose there were no artificial things like months so that we could not be mindful of the passing of time. Suppose there were no years, just the passing of hours, with no signposts to mark them into units of months and years. Then there would be no New Year.

The beginning of another year means the end of a year that has fulfilled itself and passed on. It means that some things are finished, rounded out, completed forever. It means that for some of us certain changes have taken place so profound in their nature that we can never be what we were before.

The New Year means a fresh start, a second wind, another chance, a kind of reprieve, a divine act of grace bestowed upon the children of men. It is important to remember that; whatever the fact may have been, it cannot be undone. It is a fact. If we have made serious blunders, they are made. All our tears cannot unmake them. We may learn from them and carry our hard-won lessons into the New Year. We can remember them, not with pain, but with gratitude that in our new wisdom we can live into the present year with deeper understanding and greater humanity. May whatever suffering we brought on ourselves or others teach us to understand life more completely and, in our understanding, love it more wisely, thus fulfilling God's faith in us by permitting us to begin this New Year.

II

One of the simple things that is very good and very positive about a New Year is the fact that one does have another chance, that there is available to the individual the fluid dimension of time that has not been frozen and has passed on into the past. It is liquid, living, vital, quick in the sense of being vital. The individual stands in the midst of a stream of vitality, awareness, and fluidity, and is able, by an act in the present moment, to do for him or for the context in which he is operating, something that nothing else in the world can do. Therefore when we think about the New Year, we think in terms of the sense of alternatives, the sense of option, that are still available to us. It means that all of the options are not frozen, that it is still possible to do something about a situation. Now, this is one of the very simple things.

III

The New Year means for many people a time of the making of resolutions, the time of deciding that the present and the future will be lived more intentionally than in the past, and it is important, this matter of making resolutions, because it organizes the formal intent of the personality in a given direction; it is a commitment of the individual to a performance in the future based upon an intention in the present. And this is very important. Whether the individual is able to carry out in detail the resolution—whether you are able to fulfill the thing that you intend to do—there is a clear gain in being able to bring together all of one's self in a point of focus and say that this is the thing that I intend to do tomorrow and tomorrow and tomorrow.

IV

The New Year means also the opportunity to make a revision in one's personal timetable, to look at one's life objectively, to step aside and see one's self go by, and to assess, for instance, how one spends one's time; to see how much of one's time in a twenty-four-hour period is given to the cultivation of one's own life, one's own resources; and the cultivation of those qualities which can improve the self. So often we are involved in so many activities, doing all kinds of things in response to the multitudinous pressure of the variegated demands that are made upon us, that we are somehow unable to make a little corner in our time just for ourselves and for the cultivation of our own resources against the time when we are unable to do so.

In everybody's life there should be a time out of every day when we take stock of ourselves, when we examine in a very personal and intimate way what it is that we are after, what it is that we mean with our lives, and how we are placing the emphasis on the things that we are doing.

V

One other very important thing belongs in the New Year. It is the chance to relate to something beyond our families, our cares, our responsibilities—some cause, some purpose, or some kind of human need. Suppose this year you select one thing outside the needs of your family and your responsibilities about which you will be concerned. This you try to understand and to relate to so that you will feel yourself being extended beyond the boundaries of your little world and its responsibilities.

In addition to all of the things that you are doing as a part of your responsibility as a husband or wife or daughter or what have you, there is something else, some independent something out here, some people, some causes, some purposes, something to which you will give a part of yourself. Now this may be done in terms of the repairing of fences that broke down in your relationships during the past year, so that as you move into the New Year, you will have a sense of being present and accounted for in every minute, in every hour, in every day.

The
Epilogue

In many ways beyond all calculation and reflection, our lives have been deeply touched and influenced by the character, the teaching, and the spirit of Jesus of Nazareth. He moves in and out upon the horizon of our days like some fleeting ghost. At times, when we are least aware and least prepared, some startling clear thrust of his mind is our portion—the normal tempo of our days is turned back upon itself and we are reminded of what we are, and of what life is. Often the judgment of such moments is swift and silencing: sometimes his insight kindles a wistful longing in the heart, softened by the muted cadence of unfulfilled dreams and unrealized hopes. Sometimes his words stir to life long forgotten resolutions, call to mind an earlier time when our feet were set in a good path and our plan was for holy endeavor. Like a great wind they move, fanning into flame the burning spirit of the living God, and our leaden spirits are given wings that sweep beyond all vistas and beyond all horizons. There is no way to balance the debt we owe to the spirit which he let loose in the world.

75 76 77 9 8 7 6 5 4 3 2